How to Teach Kids Anything:

Create Hungry Learners Who Can Remember, Synthesize, and Apply Knowledge

By Peter Hollins,
Author and Researcher at petehollins.com

Table of Contents

Introduction

In the distant past, intelligent and academically minded people were assumed to be natural teachers. Schoolmasters, governesses, professors, and the like were never specifically *trained* to be educators; it was enough that they understood their topic. So, before people understood that the act of teaching was itself something to learn and master, teachers were left to their own devices, helping their students arrive at knowledge and skill by whatever method they could conjure up.

Thankfully, if you're looking for more guidance than this and a more scientifically proven approach to facilitating another's learning, you have more resources than the early teachers of centuries past. In this book, we'll be carefully considering what teaching actually is, what learning is, and all the different techniques and approaches at our disposal to guide a student from where they are to where they want to be.

Education as a field has evolved and developed like any other, so expect that some of your cherished ideas about learning and how to support it will be challenged. Nevertheless, if you can follow some of the principles outlined in the chapters that follow, you will undoubtedly cultivate your own teaching prowess—and teaching is a formidable skill indeed.

Understanding the Five Types of Pedagogy

The first thing to understand: there is not just one good way of teaching.

Pedagogy can be understood as the art and science of how people learn, and consequently how we can help them by teaching. Naturally, what you consider to be learning and teaching depends on many things: how you understand the brain and the mind, how you conceive of knowledge, and the models you use to understand the way that those brains and minds interact with that knowledge. What this means is that there are multiple models, styles, approaches, or paradigms you could use.

As a teacher, you have the power to shape and direct the innate learning processes in the children you teach. Though most of us sadly undervalue the significance of a good teacher, it's amazing when you think that the quality of the relationship and understanding between you and your student literally influences the way they see and move through the world. What could be more important than that? And what could be more worth learning to do well?

The reason for becoming literate in the different ways of learning, as it were, is that you empower yourself with a large toolkit, meaning you are better able to match your approach with your student's needs. The more effectively you can do this, the better their learning will be, and the more enjoyable the experience. With the right approach, you can expect deeper engagement, more meaningful conceptual understanding, and more robust recall in the future. When you teach well, you are not just teaching the subject at hand, but also teaching your student how to learn—and the value of this skill is hard to overemphasize.

So, let's take a closer look at some of these approaches, bearing in mind that they are not just sets of techniques, but mindsets, i.e. *ways* of connecting ideas, attitudes, and techniques. One way to think of each pedagogical approach is to imagine that it's a learning environment that you construct, inside which the student learns. The more encouraging, stimulating, relevant, appropriate, and interconnected this arena, the deeper the learning.

The Constructivist Approach

If you've been to school in the last three decades, chances are that this approach was the one your teachers used, whether they knew it or not. The premise of the constructivist approach is what it sounds like: a student is assumed to learn by way of *constructing* new knowledge in their minds one unit at a time, not unlike you would build a wall one brick at a time. Starting with what you know, you gradually build and advance, incorporating new information, working methodically through categories of data, organizing yourself in a logical way. The foundations of this building are what you already know and understand.

When you teach from this perspective, then your goal is to make external structures and concepts *internal*, i.e. to embed them in the student's mind. As a teacher, you need to understand where your student is coming from (historically, culturally, and emotionally) so that you can assist them in building on those foundations, making connections, and constructing their own larger web of understanding. Students are assumed to take an active responsibility in their own learning, even though the teacher may set out a path for them to make it easier to develop through sequential steps of understanding.

To be precise, the constructivist view doesn't have "teachers" at all but *facilitators*. Your job is not to present your knowledge to a student and download your mind into theirs simply by lecturing or delivering data directly. A teacher instructs and tells, but a facilitator asks questions that suggest, hint, and shape the direction the student is already going in. With questions, dialogues, and problems, the student is placed down in a world and expected to think through learning for themselves. A good teacher supports and guides—and they can only do this if they have a thorough understanding of the path to be taken, and where the student is on that path.

In this approach, structure and context matters. Each new piece of information must be connected to prior pieces in a "scaffolding" process. Before you can learn about D and E, you need to grasp A, B, and C—and importantly, you need to know how each of these connects to one another, and the larger picture they form.

An example will make this approach clear (and indeed, using examples or analogies to illustrate a concept is a classic constructivist technique, since it uses what the student already knows to help them understand something they don't yet know). A history teacher might ask his students to make a summary of events already taught, and generate some questions or predictions about what they think will happen next. He can then shape the lesson as a task: the students essentially have to build their own lesson plan by working together to compile a summary or project that is intended to be shared with other students at their level.

Why do things this way round? When the students ask questions, think through concepts and their *meaning*, follow consequences, make summaries, and connect new information with information they already possess, they are active agents of their own learning. This is always better than being a passive receptacle of whatever the teacher is telling them. The constructivist approach is great for material that has a sequential component, or builds in logical complexity one step after another. Most textbooks imply this, where chapter nine is more difficult than chapter , and builds on the knowledge it assumes you've gathered from reading it.

The constructivist approach is not just a practical technique, though, but a set of attitudes—the facilitator in this model of teaching is attentive, supportive, and encouraging of the student's inbuilt learning drive. If the student asks them a question, they are just as likely to respond with another question, designed to prompt and cue them to the next logical unit they can add to their tower of understanding.

The Collaborative Approach

The collaborative approach is not dissimilar. If the constructivist facilitator is leveraging the student's innate ability to self-teach, then the collaborative approach takes advantage of the fact that students can and do *help each other* to learn. The classical approach has one student and one teacher. But think about how learning carries on in the "real world," outside the boundaries of formal teaching. The whole is usually greater than the sum of the parts; that is, when groups of people get together, they can often arrive at higher states of knowledge and understanding than if they had been isolated individuals.

The fundamental worldview here is that the human mind is a social object, and that dynamic critical thinking, understanding, and problem solving more naturally occur in the presence of others. Relatively modern compared to other pedagogical approaches, this view goes against the conventional image of a student working quietly alone, producing some written piece to show his understanding. Chances are your teachers heavily discouraged chatting in class in favor of having each student sit alone, at their individual desk, eyes down on their individual work!

But in the collaborative approach, interpersonal interaction is not a distraction but a powerful force to use to enhance learning. Of course, mindless chatting isn't the goal, but rather active engagement, lively debate, collective problem solving, and cooperative correction and adjustment in the group. An obvious benefit of this way of doing things is that students don't just learn dry, abstract content, but develop their communication skills, learn to self-regulate, have compassion and empathy for other students, practice cooperation and compromise, learn to argue and persuade more effectively, and gain a richer understanding of diversity of opinions and experience that are not their own (or their teacher's).

When students work in pairs and groups, they inevitably give a real-world, applied edge to the work they do. Concepts step off the page and become three dimensional and more alive. When different perspectives and varying skillsets are added as part of the learning experience, the student is broadened and works in an environment that is arguably closer to reality than hypothetical abstract situations in books.

Did you loathe group work in university? Many people did. That's because simply grouping people and jointly assigning them a task that ordinarily would be appropriate for an individual is not the same as adopting a collaborative approach (it's more likely, as you may have suspected, just a lazy way for tutors to do less work while simultaneously appearing to offer their students a so-called learning experience).

A good example of the collaborative approach in action, however, is to imagine a complex issue being assigned as a debate topic to a group of six students. There is an element of individual work, but then the students have to come together, bounce ideas off one another, and generate new questions, arguments, and concepts through their engagement.

Another example is "jigsaw" activities. Each student is given a small part of the bigger picture. Each of them is then told to construct this bigger picture, and the way to do that is through dialogue and engagement with one another. A teacher could give each student one square on a flowchart explaining a technical procedure, then ask the students to come together and imagine how the pieces fit together. You may notice that this activity is not only collaborative, but has elements of the constructivist approach, too. Finally, a basic collaborative technique is to have more knowledgeable or advanced students teach and guide less knowledgeable students. Both benefit in different ways—the former consolidate their understanding, while the latter receive a lesson from a peer who may actually understand their position better than someone who is a seasoned expert.

The Inquiry-Based Approach

A scientist or explorer doesn't need a teacher. They find their way to new knowledge and understanding on their own, right? But consider the tool they use to arrive at these new understandings: the humble question.

The question is at the heart of all learning, facilitated or not. When we are young children, even before we go to school, we do our learning with nothing more than an insatiable curiosity and the desire to understand and develop mastery of the world we find ourselves in. The constructivist approach works with the inbuilt structural characteristics of the human mind; the collaborative approach works with the inbuilt social and relational characteristics; and the inquiry-based approach gets to the heart of human curiosity, working with the fact that we naturally drive our own learning through asking questions.

To work within this pedagogical frame, the teacher must actively construct a learning environment that poses questions and problems or sets up scenarios that arouse curiosity and stimulate question-asking. The scientific method emerges when we ask questions of reality, observe the answers, adjust our hypotheses, and ask again. A simpler version of this process is what underlies learning in the inquiry-based classroom.

As you can imagine, this style of learning lends itself well to concepts in the real world that take the form of problems to be solved. What is fundamentally taught is the capacity to find solutions, and to think critically through practical, logical scenarios to arrive at understanding. The idea is that the very act of asking questions aids student understanding. It's when they actively engage with new information this way that they really cement it in their minds. They haven't just remembered some random fact, but rather they've participated with it directly, in lived experience, through questions and inquiries.

To take advantage of this natural process, a teacher can build up situations or scenarios that students have to work through. For example, a specific case study can be presented and the student asked to solve or analyze it, as is often done in legal study, clinical psychology, or even business. Or, a student can be given a very direct problem to solve—their task is not explicitly to arrive at a solution, but rather to uncover the process of solving it so they can then generalize this process to other similar problems. I'm sure you can agree this would be a much more useful approach than merely having the teacher *tell* a student, "This is how you solve it."

Here's what this approach is like in practice. Say you want to teach students basic concepts relating to the physics of floatation of buoyancy. You begin by asking them how they think massive cruise liners and ships can manage to stay afloat despite being extraordinarily heavy. After they attempt to answer the question, you explain the concepts of floatation and buoyancy by linking theory with what was said in class. However, you don't just stop there. Make your students apply what you taught them by making them design a boat that can float on water. Allow them to experiment with different materials and designs till they come up with a boat that floats. You can then further test their understanding of physics by adding weight to the boat or stimulating storms, which will make them ask more questions about these concepts so that they can improve their boat models.

Inquiry-based learning also proceeds when a teacher artfully uses questions to guide, challenge, and correct a student (we'll see more of this in later chapters). Using real-time discussions, the student can work through new material, even being prompted to devise their own questions or respond to the teacher with questions of their own. A good teacher will notice what questions the student is asking and use these to gauge their level of understanding, inferring what next step they are on the threshold of reaching, and posing questions to inspire them to get there. For example, "You have tried method A twice now, and it doesn't seem to have worked. Take a look at *why* it didn't work, though. What question can you ask now to help you understand what's going wrong?"

The Integrative Approach

In the TV show *The Wire*, a new teacher discovers with relief that he can get his ordinarily apathetic students interested in fractions and probabilities when he explains that the principles are the same as they'd use in another area of life they *are* interested in—gambling and dice games. He structures his lesson around some games of dice, and they quickly learn a few new math skills without quite realizing it.

This teacher was unwittingly using the integrative approach, where students are actively encouraged to make cross-curricula connections to enhance their learning. Again, this model rests on the acknowledgement of the fact that "in the

22

wild," humans don't learn in neat little categories and boxes, but naturally blend their understanding across different subjects.

The strength of this approach rests in the power of connections. When we connect new skills with old, or link up knowledge from multiple sources of experience, our learning is deeper and more robust. It's a little like informational triangulation: the more points of perspective you have on a single topic, the more clearly you see it. You've probably had the experience of the opposite of integrative learning at school. Maybe you learned about trigonometry in isolation, never seeing that those principles had anything to do with any other topic, even within mathematics, and never connecting that style of thinking or that knowledge with anything in life after you graduated high school.

Question: how much high school trigonometry do you remember? Probably not much! Diversity and variety is valuable. The brain evolved in a complex, dynamic, and shifting world—nothing in our natural experience comes to us in neat subject categories, perfectly cut out from the rest of life and delivered in a tidy unit. Rather, everything connects to everything else. If we want resilient, lasting and meaningful learning, we have to match our approach with the nature of information around us. We have to connect.

How far you want to take "cross-pollination" and interdisciplinary approaches is up to you. You can mix up material from two different curricula, books, or classes. You can blend concepts from two different subjects. You can use the vocabulary, ideas, and problem-solving tools from one discipline in another. You can learn using conversations, or even disagreements and points of difference. After all, many separate disciplines now exist precisely because at some point, someone decided to bring together two disparate fields of inquiry into one.

Not only does this approach help you understand and retain the information you're taking in, but it simultaneously teaches you a new skill—metathinking. This brings depth, creativity, and novelty to your learning, equipping you with the ability to think about, regulate, and direct your own learning process. This is the ultimate achievement for any student.

When applied, this approach could be as simple as a teacher asking, "What other environments do you think this process could play out in?" or, "How would a medical doctor look at the paper you've just written? Would they agree with your general thesis?"

On a deeper level, a teacher can arrange for frequent blending of different skills and subjects. Students can be asked to create a multimedia project rather than a written essay, or argue a point from the "other side" instead of their own. They could be asked to create a solution/output using an unexpected format or set of symbols. For example, students could do a project addressing a political question but approach it from a psychodynamic perspective, or do a book review in the format of a scientific paper.

The Reflective Approach

What is reflection?
When a student reflects, they are pausing to deliberately and actively engage in thinking about their own learning processes. It is in effect an act of self-appraisal and self-regulation. When we are novices, it's the teacher who plays this role, giving us feedback so that we look to them to tell us how we're doing. But the ideal situation is one in which the student themselves feels empowered to consider their performance, as well as to compare it against their own internal sense of purpose and goals. If a student can do this, as well as adjust according to what they observe, then it forms the beginning of insight . . . and learning.

Asking questions is vital to powering learning, but in a way, it's the ability to reflect, assess, and adjust that shapes and directs learning once it's begun. Experience alone is not enough. Being given feedback from the outside is better, but it's still not as good as generating your *own* form of feedback, i.e. when you are able to say,

"Hmm, what does my experience mean? What am I going to do about what I can observe about my results?"

Of all the pedagogical approaches covered here, this one is most likely to be associated with practical, hands-on learning, and is best suited to certain applied professions. For example, surgical techniques, social work skills out in the field, dance choreographies, and abilities that require mastery of an instrument or complex tool— all these things are best learned "for real" rather than in a theoretical, abstract way in textbooks. These are skills that make most sense when embedded in their natural context, and where the student can learn by doing. They can practice observing the effects of their actions, adjusting, and using the insight they gain to achieve a higher level of skill or understanding.

If you can get a student to reflect, you are handing over the learning process to them, so they take ownership of it and it becomes internalized as part of their own cognition. One general way to do this is ask them:

1. What?
2. So what?
3. What next?

For example, ask your student to analyze and describe the situation they're in, let's say by telling them to look at a circuit board they've built. They may make some analysis and assessment, but you then ask them, so what? What does this assessment mean for them? By doing so, you are triggering their reflection and asking them to evaluate and add meaning to their appraisal. The student might say they see XYZ problem with the circuit board they've built, and this means they still don't understand such-and-such concept. Then, you ask, what next? Given this analysis, what do they think should happen now? The student then directs themselves to a follow-up action. They might say they now need to revise a certain chapter again to cover some gaps in their understanding.

Students can be encouraged to engage in different kinds of reflection, even reflecting on the process of their reflection itself. As a teacher, you can ask them to look at the process they've followed, the outcome, their feelings about it, their analysis from different points of view, evaluation (i.e. is something good or bad), logical conclusions, and the gradual arrival at a plan of action. A teacher might ask students to reflect for five minutes at the end of every lesson to see what they've learned and what's still unclear, prompting them to make their own goals for the next lesson. What's important is that the teacher doesn't supply these, but encourages the student to arrive there by themselves.

Now, at this point, you're probably wondering if all these approaches are as separate as they appear when laid out here in the book. In fact, each of the approaches can be blended, modified, and extended depending on the topic, the student's strengths and weaknesses, the learning goals, and the overall context. So much the better if they are! These methods are not prescriptive, but rather tools to have in a toolkit to expand your reach in your work as a teacher. They are meant to serve your student's learning process—if they get in the way or confuse things, then they can be discarded for something that better fits your circumstances.

How to Use the Pedagogical Approaches

Naturally, having an inventory of specialized tools is only half of the solution—you still need to know when and how to use those tools. Regardless of which approaches you end up using, there are some principles of teaching that apply regardless, to all students and to all teachers, no matter what subject they are learning or at what level. We'll consider some of these principles before moving on to the rest of the book.

The first principle is that we need to think of ourselves as **facilitators, not teachers**, i.e. our job is to create a supportive environment conducive to learning, as well as create opportunities to learn. The student can and will learn—if we set up the right conditions for them. It may seem a little counterintuitive at first, but our focus should be less on the content we impart and more on the experience. Are we creating a positive, engaging, and dynamic atmosphere?

The second principle also requires a mindset shift—teaching is **not about the teacher, but the student**. Classic teaching models have the teacher front and center, dominating the experience, talking the most, and steering the lesson this way and that way. While it's tempting to get sidetracked by what *you* want students to learn, and how they should follow *your* carefully laid out lesson plan, the truth is that it should be the student and their needs at the center. If your idea of learning and the student's actual learning take two different paths, it's your job to abandon your preconceptions and support and prioritize the student's actual needs in the moment.

A third principle to keep in mind has been hinted at already in many of the above approaches: **genuine and high-quality learning is never narrow, isolated, or abstract. It's *real*.** This doesn't mean that everything you learn needs to have some physical and practical application, only that it needs to be felt as relevant to the student and their lives—otherwise, why learn it? A good teacher will constantly find ways to take the material and embed it in the real world, demonstrate it in its natural context, or apply the principles concretely. If you're teaching a language, for example, one of the best things you can do is encourage your student to engage in natural dialogues with native speakers—or at least set up a role play that mimics that natural situation; for example, ordering food in a restaurant.

No matter which pedagogical approach you use or how, you'll notice that none of them encourages the boring "teachers says stuff and student listens" model. Instead, **teaching is collaborative** and leverages relationships, both between teacher and student and between students. The teacher is never some infallible master sitting on a pedestal, delivering a pre-set lesson to the student, who passively absorbs it. Rather, teacher and student feed off each other dynamically, responding to one another, adjusting according to changing needs in the moment, and using a range of flexible tools to keep on aiming for the main goals of learning.

Whether you are in a more formal or professional teaching context, are homeschooling your own children, or would like to improve your teaching skills for some other reason, teaching is an art and a science that *requires our constant learning*. Teaching is a kind of communication, and as such, it consists of the one communicating the information, the one receiving it, and the information itself. A teacher, therefore, doesn't only have to consider the content they are trying to teach, but the way they share that message and the way it's likely to be heard.

Teaching has come a long way from its previous forms, where "teacher says stuff and student listens" was the standard approach, and the significance of things like learning styles and teacher mindset were yet to be recognized.

Takeaways

- The effectiveness of teaching depends on the characteristics of the teacher, of the student, of the material being taught, and most importantly, on the way it is taught.
- There are five main theoretical approaches to teaching called pedagogical approaches. Pedagogy is the theory and practice of teaching. No single approach is the right one—rather, it's a question of fit between the teaching style and the student, material, teacher, learning goals, context, and level of understanding.
- The constructivist approach attempts to support learning as they construct knowledge piece by piece, building on what they already know in a sequential, logical, and ordered fashion. The teacher's job is to chart an incremental course through a curriculum, promoting students to advance gradually.
- The collaborative approach takes advantage of the power of interpersonal relations to drive learning and understanding. The teacher can use collaboration, group activities,

teamwork, dialogue, or student teaching to help students grasp new concepts.

- The inquiry-based approach has the teacher set up an environment that supports and encourages the student's curiosity, using questions to spur understanding. The student is given case studies, scenarios, and problems, or simply prompted to ask or answer questions, to shape their learning process.

- The integrative approach draws connections across disciplines and subjects to deepen understanding. By cross-pollinating experience and knowledge, students develop better understanding and recall, and enjoy a more applied approach to the concepts they learn.

- Finally, the reflective approach is about encouraging the student's innate self-assessment and metacognition, i.e. thinking about their own learning so that they can self-regulate and adjust, gaining insight. Teachers can encourage this by asking students to observe their position, analyze it, and then generate their own assessments to drive follow-up actions.

- The five approaches can be blended and modified as necessary.
- The approaches all share some fundamental assumptions, namely that good teaching is inevitably collaborative, facilitative, applied, student-centered, and flexible.

Chapter 1. Teacher Mindset

Think back to your school days and try to remember who your worst teacher was, and your best. What was the difference between them?

Sadly, many people have distinct memories of awful early education experiences. They remember teachers who seemingly made their school lives hell on earth. Maybe you had a teacher who obviously hated their job and treated students with contempt or disinterest. Maybe your teacher was simply incompetent, and only succeeded in confusing the class instead of illuminating the material. Classically bad teachers are known for being antagonistic to students, clinging to outdated or frankly disastrous teaching techniques, which then take the efforts of a better teacher to undo and correct.

For many students, a bad teacher is enough to completely kill any love for a subject, no matter how good the materials are and no matter how innately talented the student is in that area. So, while most teachers may begin with wondering how they can improve their students, we'll start this chapter from a different perspective, and consider how teachers can make improvements where it really matters: in themselves.

John Hattie is a researcher deeply interested in what actually works when it comes to education. We'll look more closely at his groundbreaking research and book *Visible Teaching* in a later chapter, but for now, we'll take his approach of only considering **teaching methods that are evidence-based.** We've looked at the five broad pedagogical approaches, but Hattie wanted to quantify the effectiveness of the countless different techniques that each of these models inspired so that only the most effective could be used.

But over and above the techniques used, Hattie also claimed something you might already suspect to be true, i.e. that much of the variability in education, and the overall effectiveness of certain methods, comes down to the characteristics of the teacher and the teacher-student relationship. So, that's where we'll start.

The Six Characteristics of a Good Teacher

Hattie identified six main characteristics, and we'll explore each of them in order of most to least impactful. The first quality might come as no surprise: it's **passion**. This doesn't need too much explanation. A good teacher *wants* to teach and loves what they do. What are they passionate about? Sure, being very interested in your chosen topic is great, and that enthusiasm is naturally contagious, but a great teacher is one who is passionate specifically about helping their students learn. A teacher can be the most passionate one can possibly be about their subject, and still be a bad teacher because they don't know how to effectively impart their knowledge and curiosity onto others.

Why is passion so important? If you think about your favorite teachers growing up as a kid, maybe they possessed this characteristic in abundance. Though they certainly may have been fun-loving and energetic, what may have had the most impact is that these teachers were able to *model an optimal attitude to learning.* This is important. Children learn not just about the content you're teaching, but they also learn what mindset to adopt, and how to think and feel about that content. They learn from you how to approach not just that lesson, but learning in general.

It makes sense: if you are lackluster and uninspired about the work you are teaching, kids will observe this and correctly conclude that the work is boring and unpleasant. If you teach children that learning is an arduous, difficult process that requires force, then that's what they'll learn. If you are plodding through the curriculum with no real motivation, then how can you expect your students to find any? Passion is important, but perhaps what is most important is that we model a helpful attitude to our students. They will consciously or unconsciously adopt our own beliefs about education and learning.

For example, consider how you think about and react to failure, in yourself or your student. If your student attempts a math problem, for instance, and they get it wrong, let's say you respond by immediately mocking them and making them feel stupid for not understanding. Instead of showing them where they went wrong and guiding them toward a better answer, you dwell on the mistake and emphasize the fact that their performance is a direct reflection not of their stage in their understanding, but of their worth as human beings.

Now, you've sadly taught your student a few things: that they are stupid, that math is hard, and that there is something about them or that topic that is impossible, unpleasant, or not worth it. You have taught them to shy away from a crucial aspect of the learning process: failure. The next time you tackle a similar math problem, they may have a mental block about it, causing them to avoid it altogether or give up, not wanting to try because they don't want to fail. If making a mistake is unacceptable, then they may simply decide not to try. Many, many people decide, "I'm not good at math," for exactly this reason!

Instead, imagine a passionate teacher. Not a "fun" teacher who is all games and excitement, but one who genuinely engages with their student and helps them approach the learning process with genuine enthusiasm and curiosity. When the student gets the math problem wrong, the teacher doesn't call this a failure at all. Instead, they model an accepting, curious attitude that leads most to self-correction and insight. The teacher might say, "We've lost our way somewhere. Let's see if we can find where. Look at this second line of your work—can you tell me what you were thinking here? Let's walk through it together."

Here, the teacher is communicating something subtle but powerful—that the student, their learning, and their stage in the process is important, and that the teacher *cares* about it and is willing to support them. The teacher is showing them that making mistakes, that being a beginner—in other words, that learning itself—is safe and enjoyable. If you don't give up on the student, they don't give up on themselves.

When the teacher has passion for the process, and for the student's learning, the student can internalize this feeling and come to have faith in themselves. Eventually, enthusiasm is transferred from teacher to student—the student will spontaneously relish their own process. And isn't that a wonderful thing to give someone?

The second crucial teacher characteristic is **flexibility**. We alluded to this in the last chapter and saw that no pedagogical approach is necessarily the best, but rather that a good teacher will monitor the impact they're having on a student and adjust their approach accordingly. A good teacher should be able to adjust:

- The pedagogical approach they're using
- The particular techniques or exercises they're attempting
- The pace they're presenting those techniques
- The kind of materials used
- The way they're giving feedback
- The overall goals of learning
- Their attitude and style of communication
- And more!

You get the picture—a good teacher should be ready and able to change *everything*, so long as it ultimately serves the student's learning. Though we as teachers may have our own preferences for different techniques, and though we may personally have biases or expectations, what ultimately matters is our student's learning, and whether we are helping or hindering that learning. This means we might sometimes have to abandon a pet theory or favorite technique if it's genuinely not working for our student.

The key to doing this is being observant and regularly noticing where your student is and how they're doing. Sometimes, if we're invested in a particular lesson plan, we barge ahead with it without stopping to notice how it's being received until it's too late. Regularly pause and check in with your student. Measure your progress and theirs against your goals. Be honest if something isn't quite working out—and then commit to making small changes and checking in again. Repeat as necessary!

The attitude of flexibility can be thought of as the attitude of not clinging too hard to our own beliefs, old habits, assumptions, or prejudices. Some teachers have been working for decades, and in that time have never ventured away from the same old teaching techniques they used in their very first year in the profession. In truth, they are teachers who themselves have failed to learn anything new!

As a teacher, no matter how experienced you are, you will always be a complete novice when it comes to the complex, unique student sitting in front of you. Just as you teach your students to think critically, to develop their transferable skills, and to solve problems intelligently, *you* should approach every new lesson as an opportunity to learn something new, too, and deepen your knowledge. Constantly ask yourself, what does my student need right now for their learning? And how best can I provide that?

Maybe you notice that your student is a gregarious, empathetic personality and seems to thrive more on discussion instead of quiet writing exercises. So, you switch subtly from a constructivist approach to a more collaborative one, and engage the student in more group work and reflection. Maybe you notice your student's energy level and performance drop off regularly at around twenty minutes into the lesson, so you decide to have several shorter lessons instead of one big one. When you notice your student getting a little bored and distracted, you up the challenge or go faster, throwing them a curve ball. But you are also observing carefully to see if they're overwhelmed and confused, so you can slow down, double check comprehension, or take a break.

What is valuable in these examples is not the lesson itself, but your *responsiveness* to your student. Try to think of the lesson as a conversation—not a speech. "Listen" to your student. Present something, but observe carefully how they respond to that before moving on to the next step. Keep in mind the student's overall goals. This way, you have a yardstick to measure your progress against. Remembering that we are after evidence-based techniques, use this standard with yourself, and refuse to continue with an approach that isn't demonstrating any measurable results.

Finally, there's nothing to stop you from enlisting the student's feedback and reflection. If you're not sure how things are going, ask. Your student can tell you directly what is working and what isn't, what is aiding their understanding and what is hindering it. In the process, you also empower students to participate in their learning, rather than simply deferring to you as a master.

The third important teacher characteristic is **clarity**. To see why this is so important, simply put yourself in your student's shoes, or try to remember what it felt like to be a beginner learning something difficult for the first time. Most likely, a student sees the field of knowledge ahead of them very vaguely. Their state is one of ignorance; they may have a dim sense of what it is they are trying to learn, but the point is that they don't yet know it! Their journey is from ignorance to understanding, from confusion to clarity.

It's as though they are moving through a new terrain. You as the teacher have traveled this terrain and are familiar with the path. You need to share a map with your student to help them get to where they're going, but if your map is confusing or even incorrect, you're not going to be doing your student any favors. As such, one of the most important facets of being clear is to be able to break down information in the most basic and easily digestible blocks possible. Don't assume the student knows anything.

Clarity is not just a question of style. Being clear means being organized and focused in order to make learning as direct and easy as possible. Clarity as a teacher characteristic is about good communication and being able to focus your attention where it most matters. For example, a teacher who approaches every lesson with a conscious goal in mind, as well as a clear-cut lesson plan for how the student can achieve that goal, will naturally have more of a chance of achieving it. Being clear is like handing your student the map to the new terrain and drawing a clear line from point A to B.

If a student feels that the teacher themselves doesn't really know what they're doing, they'll feel in the dark and unconfident. Have you ever wondered why certain educational games catch students' attention so much better than other methods? Part of the reason is the clarity. In a video game, for example, the rules of engagement are crystal clear, and the student knows *exactly* what the outcome will be for certain actions they take. There is no guess work, no grey area. And it's fair—if X causes Y now, they can trust that it will cause Y later on, too.

The feedback that the game provides is instant and in direct proportion to their actions. What could be more demoralizing than working hard on something with unclear or inconsistent results, and with no firm idea of whether you're on the right track or not? When you are a teacher who communicates and engages with clarity, students always know precisely where they stand with you and with the material. They are not unclear about the "rules of the game," and even if they're still figuring a few things out, they trust in the fact that there are rules, and that somebody (i.e. you) knows how it all fits together.

We'll explore the power of clear and immediate feedback in a later chapter, but for now, it's enough to say that clarity is about focus. Before you embark on any lesson, you need to know:

- What you are learning and why
- The precise way you're going to learn it, and the steps in that process

- What is part of your lesson and what isn't, and how this lesson fits into the bigger picture
- What to do if things don't go according to plan
- How you will assess the outcome, i.e. how can you tell that learning has happened?

Even if you never explicitly discuss any of this with your student, trust that they will be able to tell if you haven't clarified these points for yourself beforehand.

A fourth teacher characteristic is the ability to form **positive interpersonal relationships** with students. It will not come as a surprise to anyone who has ever been a student, but yes, being a nice person is a big part of being a good teacher! Hattie's book, which is essentially the compiled findings of an enormous education meta-study, found that the impact of a positive student-teacher relationship has a far greater effect on student achievement than things like the teacher's training, the teacher's subject knowledge, the curriculum, or the teaching approach used. Yes, teaching method does matter, but seemingly not as much as the raw interpersonal abilities of the teacher using that method. *This is a mind-blowing insight: if we truly want to become better teachers, we need to focus most on our interpersonal skills, our communication, and our relationship with our students.*

How did the research define these interpersonal skills? It isn't rocket science. Personal characteristics such as empathy, resilience, and the ability to cooperate are an obvious asset in the classroom. When a teacher can foster a learning atmosphere that is one of mutual respect, curiosity, and kindness, students feel happier in themselves and more inspired to do their best. They feel liked and appreciated by their teachers, and may even want to impress them by working harder. They look up to their teachers in admiration and experience the whole process of learning as something they are doing *with* the teacher alongside them, rather than towering over them in judgment.

Cultivating positive interpersonal relationships isn't just something you do in class. Often, learning takes place outside the class more than it does inside of it, and as a teacher, it is incumbent upon you to help your students learn in both scenarios. Make yourself available during lunchtime or after school so that students can approach you. If possible, become involved in something besides just teaching particular subjects so that students have a chance to interact with you in different capacities, which will make them more comfortable around you. For example, you could coach a sports team at school. These are all steps you can take to nurture relationships that will be rewarding not just for your students but for you as well.

A fixed mindset is one that sees the world and the people in it as permanently what they are, i.e. meaningful change is not really possible. When a teacher has a fixed mindset, they focus on innate, unchangeable characteristics (for example, labeling students as "problem students"—a label that stays with them for years) rather than on the dynamic, fluid nature of learning and growing. A growth mindset is one that sees the world as flexible, and human beings as capable of improvement and change. Yes, innate characteristics matter, but we can also achieve with effort, and just because you did one thing yesterday, it doesn't mean you can't do a different thing today.

Good teachers don't have low expectations or personal prejudices about students since they know these can often be self-fulfilling prophecies. They don't focus on ego, but on performance and development. They never say, "You're wrong; you're a failure," but instead say, "This answer isn't right"—only the latter makes learning feel safe to students.

A teacher needs a growth mindset because it's this attitude that's most aligned with an obvious form of growth: learning. Teachers also need adaptability, confidence in themselves, a sense of humor, good boundaries, the ability to listen, humility, and a genuine affection for their students. A teacher is always communicating, whether they are aware of it or not. You are not only teaching your student about the lesson at hand, but you are teaching them about who you are, how to see themselves as people, how to learn, how to deal with challenge and adversity, how to set goals, how to take responsibility, and what attitude to take to their own strengths and limitations. One excellent way to use interpersonal skills to guide your student is through good quality feedback, which we'll consider in more detail in a later chapter.

There are no quick fixes for how to foster a good relationship with your student. It takes time, and it has to be genuine. Even if you find yourself having very little in common with them (or actively dislike them!), you still have the opportunity to model respect and kindness. You can still show interest in them as people, work with them, and listen to what they have to say. A teacher-student relationship is still a relationship, and as such, it depends on *reciprocal* understanding and good communication.

Your role as a teacher could be understood more along the lines of coaching, where you and the student work together to help achieve their goals. Remember that above all, your student is a human being with fears and hopes, strengths and weaknesses, a history and a future. Connect authentically with them as the human being that *you* are, and you may find yourself becoming a better teacher without ever picking up a book on teaching methodologies.

A fifth characteristic of a good teacher is **pragmatism**, or in other words, the commitment to only using teaching strategies that are evidence based. This is in line with Hattie's central thesis, which is that if we want to be good teachers, we need to be honest and hold ourselves to a high standard, using only those techniques we can be sure have a measurable positive effect on the people whose learning we are in charge of. This takes some of the other characteristics already listed—clarity to see how you're currently doing, flexibility to consider practical alternatives, and the passion to always keep striving to do better.

It's tempting to stick with what you know, or to keep going with an approach because you think it *should* work or you would like it if it did work, rather than it actually working. But you need to be rigorous with yourself and regularly appraise the effect you are actually having on your student. It wouldn't be enough to send a child to school and hope they were learning something along the way, without ever devising a way to verify what they'd learned or see if they'd improved. So, don't allow yourself to do this as a teacher.

Another aspect of being pragmatic as a teacher is being able to communicate your decisions, particularly with regard to testing, to your students effectively. We all probably remember having teachers who seemed to do whatever they wanted based on their whims and fancies. They'd grade you harshly for no apparent reason, use teaching techniques that appeared to be counter-productive, or be unreceptive to certain ideas during class discussions because they hadn't engaged with them before. Behaving in this manner lowers your credibility in the eyes of the student and makes it much less likely that they will want to learn from you. As Stephen Brookfield has pointed out, credibility is one of two main factors that determines how effective you'll be as a teacher. If you don't exercise pragmatism and take the time to communicate effectively with students, you run the risk of becoming one of the bad teachers you yourself might've despised early in your life.

As part of your own self-reflection, practice a little humility when it comes to your own teaching so you can honestly look at what you've done well and what could be improved upon. This is where a growth mindset and flexibility come in most handy. Practice, for example, admitting to your students when you genuinely don't know the answer to a question, or owning up to a mistake you've made. If you can say things like, "You know what, I think you're right about this and I've been mistaken," then you not only demonstrate to your students just how to carry themselves with dignity, you also give yourself the opportunity to be better. Isn't this the spirit of learning you want to convey to your student?

Connected to this characteristic is a teacher's ongoing **desire to improve** their teaching. Some young people dream of being teachers when they grow up because they quite like the idea of being "the boss" and being right, wielding a red pen and making the rules, and so on. Even for adults, it can be an appealing idea to imagine being in that powerful position, enjoying being deferred to as an arbiter of learning, being in charge, and seldom questioned when incorrect. These are often the teachers that finish their training and assume that, forever after, they are experts on education and know best.

The truth is, however, that teachers who aim for this position of infallibility and power are often the least effective, because they do not constantly keep on top of their own development. Because they are unable to challenge their long-held biases or bad habits, these get embedded into their personalities and teaching styles, never being updated or improved upon. A good teacher, however, is always willing to be a student. No matter how much they learn, they know they can learn more. They are not afraid of acknowledging where they could improve, or where they may have gotten a little complacent or lazy in their approach.

A good teacher reads widely and undergoes regular training, formal and informal, to fine-tune their craft. They seek out and seriously consider opposing views, rather than assuming they already know everything. They ask for help from other teachers, and welcome reviews and feedback from their students (something that takes a lot of nerve and self-confidence!). They collaborate with others rather than working alone, because they know that other teachers can help them improve and teach them something new.

Thinking back to some of your favorite schoolteachers again, can you see how they exemplified some or all of these characteristics? As teachers, we strive to impact the inner worlds of our students. But the irony is that we can best do this by thinking carefully about our *own* mindsets first, and making sure we are approaching students and the lesson with the right attitude. If teacher mindset is so important, does this mean it's useless to think about strategy? Of course not. But as we move on to the rest of the book and turn our attention to these various strategies, it's worth bearing in mind that they will be far, far more effective when combined with the optimal mindset.

Takeaways

- John Hattie is an educational researcher whose meta-study aims to find the most effective teaching approaches and methods. This focus on evidence-based teaching is grounded in what has greatest benefits for student learning.
- Hattie found that there were six main characteristics associated with good teachers and good student outcomes.
- Passion for students' learning was by far the most important, and entailed a teacher being genuinely enthusiastic in the process of learning and their subject, which rubs off on students and inspires them to learn.

- Flexibility is also important, since it allows teachers to adapt and adjust to their unique students and their changing needs. A good teacher can observe the results of the lesson and change the pace, pedagogical approach, activities, tone, or feedback style accordingly, for their students' benefit.
- Clarity is what allows teachers to outline and communicate a clear, logical learning path for the student, and communicate this so that the student always knows what, why, and how they are learning. Clarity in feedback and expectations can make students feel secure and confident in their path.
- Good teacher-student relationships are also essential. A teacher needs to have a genuine human connection with the student, and convey empathy and understanding. Like any relationship, it needs to be built on mutual respect, trust, and good communication.
- Good teachers are pragmatic and use only evidence-based teaching strategies. They are willing to learn, adjust, or try new things when old techniques aren't

working. They hold themselves to high standards.

- The final characteristic is the desire and willingness to improve our teaching skills. A good teacher knows never to rest on their laurels, but to keep learning, keep refining their approach, and to work with other teachers to improve themselves continually.

Chapter 2. General Principles for Teaching and Educating

In the previous two chapters, we examined the broad pedagogical approaches teachers can take, as well as the basic characteristics that great teachers usually possess. In a way, we have now equipped ourselves with the primary colors of teaching. In this chapter, we'll now be looking at how to mix these colors to create more complex shades, and how to paint a more elaborate picture using what we know so far.

The Goldilocks Principle

You know the story—Goldilocks tried Papa Bear's porridge and found it too hot. Then she tried Mama Bear's porridge and found it too cold, but when she tried Baby Bear's porridge, she found it just right. The Goldilocks zone of learning is that sweet spot where a student learns best—not too difficult, not too easy, but just right.

The trouble with mainstream schooling is that it's unlikely that all thirty-odd students in a classroom have exactly the same definition of "just right." Some kids will find a certain exercise boring, while others will be overwhelmed and get frustrated. A few may get in the "zone" and learn something. A student may experience learning as distressing and confusing, constantly feeling unable to step up to the task, and constantly feeling stupid as a result (i.e. it's too difficult). Other students might see learning as a dreary, boring slog that's about as exciting as pulling teeth. They feel squashed down, uninterested, and distractable (i.e. it's too easy). A teacher ideally wants their student to fall right between those two extremes, where challenge is pitched at just the right level.

Take a look at how your student responds to the experience of not understanding something. Perhaps they feel energized and motivated, suddenly roused by curiosity or inspired to go out seeking answers, figuring out the puzzle, or beating the odds. But perhaps they feel differently, and see this experience as primarily a negative one, where they feel embarrassed, self-conscious, ashamed, or simply stressed out. Just like you, your student has a unique threshold and ways of thinking about challenge when it comes to learning.

As a teacher, part of your job is to keep alive your student's natural and innate love of learning—whatever that looks like for them. This means we need to be aware of how they are experiencing the learning process. We need to pitch the level of our lessons so that the student experiences a process that is **difficult yet satisfying**. So, we need to understand *their* definitions of difficult and satisfying.

How do you know where this level is, though? Research done in 2019 by Wilson and colleagues in *Nature Communications* puts the magic number at eighty-five percent. We learn best when we are doing a task where we can expect around an eighty-five percent accuracy rate. This puts us at the outer edge of our current abilities without leaving us completely bewildered and demoralized.

In practice, you might give a student an exercise to do and notice that they achieve a one hundred percent score on it, meaning it's probably too easy for them and you risk boring them or losing their attention. So, you increase the difficulty and see how they do. If you knock them up three levels and they're suddenly only averaging thirty percent correct answers, you've gone too far and need to pull back to more familiar territory again.

Another version of the Goldilocks rule is called the Yerkes-Dodson law, which describes a non-linear relationship between arousal and performance. This model was outlined in 1908 by Robert Yerkes and John Dodson and used experiments with rats to conclude that increasing stress and arousal levels increase performance—but only up to a point.

Arousal here refers to cognitive stimulation, excitement, activity, or, if you like, stress.

Initially, as arousal increases, so does performance. For example, your boss keeps putting more tasks on your to-do list, and so you keep stepping up to meet the demands. But after a while, you reach a peak of performance beyond which you start to perform worse. From this point on, increases in arousal actually brings steadily worsening performance. So, if your boss keeps on assigning tasks well after you've reached your peak, you may actually start to make mistakes or perform poorly.

Naturally, it takes a longer time to reach this peak performance point when the task is easy, and we reach that point sooner when the task is more difficult. The important thing, however, is that no matter what the task is or how skilled we are, there is a definitive optimal peak at which we are performing maximally at the highest level of challenge. Below this peak, the task is too easy, and above it, the task is too hard. But right in between—the Goldilocks zone.

How can you use this idea to help your students? Here's where your six great teacher characteristics come in. You'll need to appreciate that no two students are alike, and that what most matters is that you understand your student's experience from their point of view. That means that a particular exercise, task, or piece of information is not difficult or easy in itself. It only becomes so if a student experiences it that way.

You will only notice this if you take the time to observe where they actually are. Keep the eighty-five percent rule in mind and adjust as you go. You are watching to see if your student is operating at the fringe of their abilities, but you also want to pay attention to their emotional state. Are they feeling demoralized, doubtful, or unconfident? Confused? Or just bored? A student may be answering all the questions correctly but nevertheless find the experience stressful and unpleasant. In this case, you may still wish to dial back the challenge somewhat until the student feels *emotionally* up to the task, even though they are already *cognitively* able to do it.

Use ample student reflection and pay attention to your student's energy levels, motivation, and mood. Notice the kinds of mistakes they are making—it's a good sign if the quality of mistake is actually improving, whereas you should ease off if the student is making mistakes simply because they are flustered, confused, or feeling rushed. Try to reduce your students' cognitive overload wherever necessary, especially while teaching complicated concepts. Provide key takeaways and teach around them. The ones who aren't as motivated can survive on the takeaways, while those who are can learn further. Our personal sense of competency develops alongside our capacities. Keep this in mind and let your students develop their confidence and skill in tandem, step by step.

Even when following the eighty-five percent rule, you can also consider evenly balancing out challenge with achievement. For example, try not to have too many ultra-difficult questions one after the other. Throw in the occasional problem you know your student can manage, to keep their confidence and engagement up. They need to feel like they are advancing, but it can be useful to have one hand still holding on to the safe and familiar as they do so.

A particularly tricky challenge you may encounter while trying to implement the Goldilocks principle is to accommodate children with special needs. When trying to teach such students, the most important thing to do is to not treat them as if their learning capabilities are any different from the other children. Having said that, you can cater to them in some specific ways without singling them out. So, when trying to test your students, design multiple tests that challenge students in different ways and let them choose which method they prefer to be tested in. You can also give special needs children extra attention outside of class and help them understand concepts by providing additional resources and using a mixture of the pedagogical approaches we outlined above. All of this is undoubtedly extra work for you, but it can make someone feel special and completely change their approach to learning for the rest of their life.

The Heick Learning Taxonomy

In the previous section, we spoke about dialing up or down the difficulty of a task as though this were a trivial thing. For some subjects, this is pretty easy to do—for example, longer words are generally harder to spell than shorter ones, so spelling is easy enough to grade on a scale of easy to difficult. But chances are your chosen topic is not so straightforward, and it's difficult to say which piece of knowledge is more fundamental than another.

A more pressing issue with teaching is this: how do you know when your student has actually understood? If you know your student "gets" something, then you can move on to something more challenging—but how do you know they genuinely get it?

The trouble is that students can learn to give you the answers they think you want to hear, without those answers being genuine and spontaneous reflections of the understanding they've gained. Even worse, sometimes a student doesn't even know that they don't know, so they certainly can't convey to this to you. Students' brains are like black boxes—we can't look to see what's inside, but have to infer what's in there based on what they share and communicate with us.

The following model—a learning "taxonomy"—is a particularly useful tool when it comes to assessing understanding. In any teaching endeavor, you are working on three main principles: you need to know what your student needs to understand (the goal and standard you're aiming for), you need to know what they understand right now (assessment) and how to get them from where they are to where they need to be (this is where your teaching strategy comes in).

Heick's taxonomy is a list of isolated tasks that increase in complexity. The idea is that if you can complete these tasks, you can demonstrate understanding, i.e. the student's head is no longer a black box, and you can determine whether they've grasped something and, if not, at which level their understanding has reached. Each level of understanding depends on the previous level. You can run this taxonomy quickly and without too much effort, and use your insight into the student's understanding to adjust your lesson. Then, you don't risk a nasty surprise later on when a formal assessment or test reveals a lack of understanding where you genuinely thought the student was on the same page as you!

In the taxonomy, there are six domains of cognition to move through. Let's consider each with an example, to show how you might use them during lessons.

Domain 1 – The Parts

At the most basic level, students can be said to understand if they can identify and recognize the different components that make up the topic they're learning about.

- Describe the topic in your own, simple words
- Label the major and minor parts
- Decide which are the most and least important aspects

- Take the idea or item apart to see its elements
- Find examples of the principle, and identify what doesn't count as an example
- Put the topic in a broader category, or break its components down into categories

As an example, imagine you are teaching your students about the respiratory system. Before you could determine their understanding on the function of the lungs etc., you could assess their understanding at the most basic level, in domain 1. You could ask them to label a diagram of the lungs and identify all the different structures and features, as well as identify the parts most responsible for the lung's main functions. You could Look at the different airways and ask the student to categorize them, for example according to size or what other organs they connected to.

You could simply pause somewhere in your lesson, after introducing an overview of the respiratory system, and ask the student to explain the idea back to you, but in their own words. You might explain the most basic principles of how the heart connects to the lungs and the main purpose of the lungs, and then ask the student to sketch this out to show they've understood. You could also ask the student to identify other bodily systems (i.e. digestive, circulatory) as a way to categorize the lungs broadly, or else ask them to "take apart" the lung by drawing one magnified portion or imagining a structure opened up or with layers peeled away to reveal what's underneath.

Domain 2 – The Whole

As you do the above, your student will naturally arrive at the next level of understanding, which is to grasp how all the separate elements come together, and the bigger whole they form.

- Explain the topic both in minute detail and in the "bigger picture" view
- Embed the idea or image in a broader context

- Explain different ways this idea or item is useful, both physically and intellectually
- Play with it to get a deeper sense of the entire concept
- Use it in part or as a whole to work on something else, as a tool
- Make changes and updates to it

Once your student understands the parts that make the whole, they are able to understand the whole as a whole. For example, you can give your student exercises that ask them to zoom in and out of the anatomy of the lung, or see the parts not just as parts, but as steps in a process called respiration. You could ask them to complete a table with columns for "structure" and "function" and then test their comprehension by asking what they think would happen if the structure was changed in some way. The idea is to test whether students have now understood the topic in question in more exhaustive detail than they did in the previous domain. You can do this through any of the pedagogical approaches outlined earlier. Ask students questions or integrate concepts with breathing in different scenarios like during exercise and at rest.

If your student has seen that the lung's structure seems to prioritize surface area, you can then ask your student why they think this is, and what role that surface area plays in the body. You could ask the student to imagine how certain injuries or illnesses might compromise this function—and their answer can tell you whether they are capable of understanding the lungs as a functional whole. Push your student's understanding of concepts by introducing unforeseen variables that challenge what they've just learned and force them to think out of the box to account for these variables. By doing this, you can ensure that your students truly understand the whole because it will be much harder for them to fake it.

Domain 3 – Interdependence

At some point, it comes down to connections again! Your student has a higher level of understanding when they can begin to grasp that the topic they are learning about connects to plenty of other topics. How can you assess whether they've reached this level of understanding? Try asking your student to do one of the following:

1. Connect the idea to other similar or completely dissimilar ideas
2. Compare and contrast to other ideas
3. Practice "teaching" what you know to others
4. Write explanations for this idea pitched at both a novice and an expert level
5. Explain misconceptions or common points of misunderstanding
6. Find analogies to other ideas, concepts or arguments

You might be teaching your student about the history of communism in Russia. To test that they're really following along, you could regularly ask them to write essays or short explanations about how communism compares to other political and economic ideologies. If they can home in on the defining features of communism that make it different from all other governmental systems, then you know they understand them. You could also ask them to compare communism in Russia with communism in other countries such as China so that they understand the nuances of the ideology even among those who ascribe to it. By doing this, you're ensuring that they can compare ideas that are similar as well as dissimilar to each other.

You could ask the student to give you a little presentation or speech where they have to teach you. Mix this up by asking the student to not just explain it at their level (i.e. imagining they're addressing a fellow student) but that they have to convey the concepts to those who are complete beginners. The easiest way to implement this is to make it a group activity so that they're not just teaching you but also fellow students. Pair up a student you know has understood the concept well with someone who might be struggling with it. Since students are more attuned to each other's needs, this may be much more productive than simply having them teach the concepts to you, someone who already knows a lot on the topic. The idea is that if you cannot explain a concept in its most basic terms to a person who is completely new to them, then you don't truly grasp the concepts yourself.

Domain 4 – The Function

This cognitive domain tests your student's ability to see the concept *in action*. Ask them to:

- Apply the concept in familiar and unfamiliar situations
- Describe its function using analogies
- Describe its ideal function and how to get most utility out of it
- Find unexpected and creative ways to use it
- Analyze when to use it, and why
- Think about its invention or creation, and make a theory about its origins

No idea, concept or theory is completely static. Students gain deeper understanding when they can not only see the whole, its parts and how they connect, but also how they function in the broader environment, and what this means for them. Staying with Russian communism, ask your student to consider if the same principles could be applied in other countries or historical periods, and ask them to explain why or why not. Give them creative scenarios like how being a communist country surrounded by non-communist ones will impact the former, or how international bodies like the UN will deal with a communist country despite following fundamentally different principles.

Ask them if they can imagine new and creative ways to use the principles of communism, or about how the philosophy might change depending on who practiced it and why. Finally, ask them to imagine why this political and economic ideology developed in the first place—can they imagine the *function* that this worldview played for its adherents, not just socially but politically? Your students' answers will reveal a lot—if they are unable to make conceptual manipulations, or turn the concept round in their minds, then it's likely that their understanding is still on the structural levels below.

Domain 5 – The Abstraction

Before we continue, it's worth noting that not all students, and not all subjects, need to be carried out to their highest level of understanding. Depending on your learning goals, your student's ability level and personality, and the stage you are in your curriculum, you can pitch your questions at a particular level and no further. This is where your own understanding comes in handy—you cannot correctly facilitate and asses your student's understanding if you are shaky in your own! To assess a more abstract insight into any material, see if your student can:

- Deal with the topic's nuances
- Apply critical thinking to the topic and analyze it closely
- Debate it, including consider the opposite viewpoint to their own

- Analyze it in terms of objectivity and subjectivity, fact and opinion
- Analyze it in terms of style, elegance, relevance, and so on
- Create a follow up or extension, a sequel, a rebuttal or an evolution

A student who is operating at this level of understanding can grasp not only the surface features of a concept and its function, but the very meaning behind it, and the way that meaning has been constructed. If you are working through a piece of historical literary fiction with your student, you could test their depth understanding by asking them to tell you what they think of the themes, plot, style etc. over and above the simple narrative outline.

Do they like the book? Can they argue their opinion convincingly? How would they improve it or can they imagine writing their own version of this tale, with a twist? Perhaps you ask them to think about the author and their intentions, and think critically about these. Ask students to situate the author in the socio-historical scenario in which they wrote this story and how contemporary beliefs may have impacted how the novel turned out. Students who find these questions disorienting, or who continue to default to more concrete explanations, are likely not at this level of cognition.

Domain 6 – The Self

For most subjects, domain 5 is more than sufficient, and this is the limit most often reached in high school or university level learning. Recalling the reflective pedagogical approach, we can take the student's abstract and theoretical understanding one step further and ask them to consider themselves and how they relate to the learning process. See if your student can:

- Devise their own plan for future learning
- Ask you questions to guide their own learning
- Appraise and assess their learning journey critically

- Apply what they've learned in a range of contexts, even outside of your prompts
- Correctly identify gaps in their own learning and devise a plan to fill them
- Evaluate their self-knowledge and look reflexively at their own understanding

At this level, the classic "student has become the teacher" moment is achieved, and the student comes to see themselves and their own learning in a clear light. This awareness naturally empowers students to make active choices for themselves, and you may find that they spontaneously demonstrate this level of understanding without you having to ask them. Rather, they will ask you, or they will consciously drive their learning in a specific direction, or else offer up analysis of their performance that resembles what you would provide.

This stage of the process can be very mutually rewarding for both, the student and the teacher. As the teacher, you can assess the way they've learned and where there are still gaps in their understanding of ideas and use it as feedback for when you teach the topic to a different batch of students. Even though everyone learns differently, having one student's input when they've reached this level of understanding can help you optimize your teaching to a significant degree. For the student, asking them to devise their own methods of teaching the same concept and outlining a plan for them to continue learning themselves can expose patterns where your student struggles. Maybe they can understand ideas but not apply them to tricky scenarios. This can enable them to devote extra focus to their weaknesses, and also help you strengthen yours.

Clear Communication and Dissemination

Ok, so you've gauged your student's level of understanding using the above framework and a few pointed questions . . . and you've discovered that despite your best efforts, the student still has no idea what you're talking about. Now what?

Your student's conceptual grasp depends on their own history, their abilities, and even their age. But the biggest and most relevant factor influencing their understanding is the quality of *your explanation*. If you take the time to understand where the student needs to be, and where they currently are, you can craft an explanation to help them cross that distance more effectively. To explain things effectively, you need to have a good understanding of concepts, what they are, and how to communicate them.

Concepts are tools. They help us explain, analyze, define, and identify the data in the world around us so we can make sense of it.

When we understand something and have knowledge of it, it's the *concepts* we have grasped. So, to teach, our work comes down to communicating concepts. Concepts can either be sensory (i.e. concretely detected by our sense organs) or abstract (perceived by the intellect, logic, or rationality). The very first step is to understand what kind of concept you are trying to explain. Knowing how to hold a calligraphy pen is more of a sensory concept, whereas the relationship between a written word and its referent is a more abstract concept.

What follows is a broad two-step process to try when planning a way to explain new concepts to your student.

Step 1: State and Define

The first thing you need to do is to establish the context and goal of learning. State clearly what it is you're trying to convey to your student. Identify whether it is a sensory or abstract concept, then define what exactly it is you're talking about. Your statement or definition makes a claim on the class and category that thing belongs to, and this tells us about its characteristics. This in turn helps you distinguish and identify the thing you're focusing on.

For example, "Ragtime was a popular musical style that emerged in the 1890s amongst black Americans. It can be recognized by its syncopated 'ragged' rhythms in two-four or four-four time, with melodic accents between the beats." This tells you what ragtime *is* (a kind of music) and also what makes it unique (its syncopated rhythm with melodic accents). In a way, a good definition tells you what a thing is, and also what it isn't.

Think of this first step as an orientation to your student—a "you are here" arrow on the map that contextualizes and delineates what you're going to explain to them. "Today, we are going to learn about present perfect tense, which is a tense in English that is primarily used to show activity that occurred in the past but is still continuing today, or could continue."

The way you state and define a concept at the outset will be key to how much attention students pay over the course of you covering this topic. If it appears to be something complicated and difficult, they might be demotivated and discouraged from engaging with it as closely as they would if they found the idea or concept to be more approachable. Make sure you state the concept in very simple, easily understandable terms and make use of examples so that students can relate it to something practical or connect it to something they already know. This is discussed in greater detail ahead.

Step 2: Use Examples, Elaboration, and Analogies

Now that you've set a definition and stated the parameters, you can refer to your new concept by using concepts your student is already familiar with. This returns to the idea of the constructivist approach, where we build new concepts on the foundations of old ones. When you give a definition, it's a little like having your student understand the features or parts that make up a concept—but it doesn't tell them much more. To make this definition come alive, however, you need to apply it somehow to the student's reality.

Find the key attributes of your concept and link it to pre-existing concepts. The easiest way to do this is by making an analogy, for example, "Ragtime sounds a little like the old-timey music they'd play in a saloon in a classic Western movie, or what you'd hear in the background of an old silent film. It's played on a piano, but the piano always seems to sound a little out of tune!"

The previous definition of ragtime might have been technically true, but it's not a lot for a person to grab a hold of. You need to go a little further. Giving analogies can instantly add color and understanding to your explanation. For very concrete or sensory concepts, you could literally perform or demonstrate the concept to make your point—such as humming the famous ragtime tune "The entertainer," which most people instantly recognize and understand far quicker than a dry musicological explanation.

It's remarkable that human beings learn and understand what a thing is by essentially learning what it is *like*, but analogies and metaphors have always been powerful ways to communicate and explain what we mean. Construct analogies that will help your student understand the category the thing belongs to, and its features. This could also mean saying what it isn't, and what groups it doesn't belong to and why. "It's a bit like jazz piano except not improvised and more regular, and it's definitely not like classical piano because it's fair simpler, more rhythmic, and syncopated."

One of the best ways to make your point is to use an example—in fact, a great teaching technique is to start with an example, and go from there, perhaps leading your student with some questions that point them towards defining characteristics. Perhaps you share three pieces of writing and ask them what they think they each have in common. By asking your student to uncover these categories and definitions for themselves, they'll gain a deeper understanding than if you had merely provided them. Alongside examples, you might also want to make use of non-examples. As the name suggests, this is the exact opposite of an example, illustrating a situation or scenario where something doesn't fit. So, if you share three pieces of writing, compare commonalities as well as differences. This will help students compare as well as contrast, leading to more holistic learning.

You could try using case studies or hypothetical situations, or else show instances where the concept plays out so students can see it and all its possible variations. "Here's how they used this ELISA assay to diagnose HIV infection," or, "This particular battle clearly shows Sun Tzu's *Golden Bridge* military strategy being used, and one of its possible outcomes." Try role plays or work through example dialogues or problems, and consider comparing a "right way" and "wrong way" approach so your student understands *why* a certain method is ideal.

In the first step, you are being didactic, i.e. you are simply instructing your student and telling them what's what. But in the second step, your explanation really comes to life. Here, you make efforts to package this new piece of information in a way that your student can hear and process. Reach into their memory and past experience to help them draw connections between *that thing* and *this thing*. Not only does this bootstrap comprehension, it also creates a psychological feeling of familiarity, making new ideas seem less intimidating and strange.

If you're not sure what analogies, metaphors, or links you can offer your student, try the following:

- Consider what has helped you make that "aha!" moment in the past, when you were learning about this concept for the first time.
- Think about what has allowed your student to have breakthroughs in the past. If you know that things always "click" for them when put in a graphic or diagrammatic form, for example, start there.
- Look closely at the new concept and try to identify its most important and relevant feature. Now, try to think of other concepts that possess this same feature. For example, in teaching the complicated concept of electricity, you can refer heavily to metaphors of water flows and rivers, which the student will undoubtedly be more familiar with. Later, once electricity is understood, you can even use the

concept of the flow of electricity to explain an even higher-order concept, like electromagnetism.

- Appeal not only to your student's memories and existing knowledge, but to their unique background, their unique perspective, their interest and beliefs, and their personality. Analogies and explanations that register with the emotions are far likelier to stick than more academic ones.

In the spirit of this section itself, here are some examples to illustrate how to weave in useful explanations in your teaching:

- "The hypothalamus is like a switchboard operator in the brain, and hormones are like the messages it sends throughout the rest of the body to regulate all sorts of processes."
- "In gothic literature, the *pathetic fallacy* is a narrative technique where the described weather matches the characters' internal emotional state. For example, using thunder and

lightning to signify the heroine's distress and fear."

- "ATP is like a currency but for energy. Every time you break this bond right here, it's like you are spending one unit of this currency to power something."
- "If the sun were a grapefruit, the earth would be the size of a pinhead, fifteen meters away."
- "*Kafkaesque* is an adjective derived from an author's name, just like *Orwellian*."
- "This idea was little like a Grand Unified Theory of everything, but for the art world."
- "Dorothy Parker was like a female Oscar Wilde."
- "We can think of the new techno-elite as a twenty-first century aristocracy, and of participation in the gig economy as a form of modern-day serfdom."

Using examples, analogies and metaphors in your explanations takes practice, an understanding of your student, and a sufficiently deep grasp of the topic you're trying to teach. The more analogies you can use, the better, since this gives your student a more three-dimensional view on the same topic, seen from many different angles. If an analogy doesn't work, it doesn't mean that you or your student have done something wrong. Don't keep on with the same explanation, though; switch it up and try something else. You may find that in explaining things in different ways, you yourself gain a richer understanding of the concept, or uncover some of your own misunderstanding!

Logical Fallacies and Critical Thinking

As you guide your student to a more sophisticated understanding of the new material in front of them, the hope is that eventually, they no longer need your facilitation—they can undertake the same process for themselves. A good teacher is able to help a student grasp a new topic or idea, but a great teacher knows how to teach a student *how to learn* so that they can comfortably tackle any new topic going forward.

Your lesson can be thought of as training wheels, but eventually, your student needs to ride that bike alone, without your prompting and support. We've seen that as a teacher, you model a particular attitude and approach to learning (and to failing!) but you also model how to think in general, in the way you lay out your lesson plans, and the exercises you assign.

For almost all students, the art of critical thinking is a vital and non-negotiable skill, not just for academic life but for life in general. A great general principle to focus on as you teach your student is to regularly foster their ability to think about what they're doing, and to make conscious evaluations of not just the *content* of their thoughts, but the *quality* of those thoughts. The greater their critical thinking skills, the more competent they will be at directing and assessing their own learning—i.e. you will have done your ultimate job as a teacher.

To get better at critical thinking, we need to consistently be aware of and guard against logical fallacies that undermine the quality of our thought processes. To help our students get better at critical thinking, we need to be on the watch for these logical fallacies in them, so we can help them become aware of them, and find alternatives. You can combine work on logical fallacies with self-reflection—i.e., ask your student to regularly consider *how* they are thinking and not just *what* they are thinking.

There are many logical fallacies, and interested teachers can read up on the more exotic ones if they like, but here we will explore only the most common ones:

Ad Hominem Fallacies

This is essentially when a student muddles the *source* of the argument with the argument itself, i.e. instead of engaging with the premises of a presented argument, they focus on the person making the argument. So, if someone the student disagrees with in general says something that is factually correct, they may falsely disagree with that information because the assumption is more or less, "the person and their argument are the same."

People do this all the time: a good-looking actor is sometimes assumed to be talking sense when they weigh in on political or current events, because people mistake their liking for the actor for an evidence based argument or claim. Or a person decides that because Hitler was a totally evil human being, that *all* of his ideas and theories were wrong, and that it's simply not possible to agree with any proposition he made.

One form of ad hominem fallacy is called "guilty by association," where we judge a person based on the company they keep rather than on who they are as people. We might assume that someone whose family members have been involved in crime are necessarily less trustworthy, or that people who belong to a religion associated with terrorism must also be terrorists, simply by association.

Another example is to attack or disagree with a claim not because of what it is, but because of where it comes from. Many people will refuse to accept a logical and sound argument if it comes from their opposing political party or from a social group they disagree with on other topics. For example, a man might make a valid criticism about feminism, but his argument may be dismissed because he is a man and not a woman. The logical and rational thing to do would be to look at the people, the arguments they make and the actions they choose in isolation, and consider them on their own virtues. While these knee-jerk reactions and prejudices may occasionally be true, consciously removing this fallacy from your cognitive repertoire will undoubtedly improve the quality of your thinking.

How can we discourage this fallacy in the classroom?

As with all logical fallacies, a great way to heighten your student's awareness is to use targeted questions that challenge their assumptions. Essentially, you can use what's called the Socratic method to force your student to slow down and look more closely at how they are thinking. You may recognize the Socratic method as a form of inquiry-based learning, where questions are used to direct the learning process.

Questions can be used for all the fallacies we'll consider shortly, and can take many forms. Whatever kind of question you ask, however, you should keep in your mind that questions are there as signposts, hints, clues, or cues. Think about what you want your student to understand, then pose a question to bring their attention to that point. Simply telling students not to commit the fallacy or to keep it in mind while thinking critically will likely not work because our biases can be very deep rooted. As such, it's advisable to keep "instructing" to a minimum and force students to think for themselves by asking thought-provoking questions that challenge their presumptions.

For example, let's say your student is reading some text written by a seventeenth-century monk and decides that his opinions about life are irrelevant since he lived so long ago and couldn't possibly understand anything. In other words, they look at the text and conclude that the arguments made are flawed simply because of *who* is making those arguments. You could ask:

Probing questions: "So are you saying that humans were fundamentally different then than they are now?"

Inductive questions: "If this monk doesn't know what he's talking about, does it mean that you are not allowed to have an opinion about something you haven't experienced yourself?"

Open-ended questions: "What do you think it would be like if you had to share your opinion with people living hundreds of years in the future. Would you agree if they told you that you knew nothing because you lived in a different era to them?"

Clarifying question: "Are you saying that this argument is wrong *simply because* it was an old monk who made the argument? Would you agree if a modern day person made the same claims?"

The Strawman Fallacy

In a strawman argument, someone is attacking or engaging not with their opponent's claim or position, but with a "strawman"—a distorted, overly simplified, or inaccurate version of their argument. A strawman is not a real man, and a strawman argument is not a real argument. Rather, it's something that's more easily defeated, and as such is a strategy that is not in good faith.

This sort of fallacy is often employed in politics, where the opposing view is blown out of proportion, twisted, minimized or demonized until it doesn't resemble anything the opponent has actually claimed. For example, side A claims that abortion should be free and legal, and side B says, "Look at Side A over there; they hate children and want to end family life for everyone." If one person says they don't agree that teachers should announce their sexual orientation to the children they teach, another person may say, "Ah, so your opinion is that you hate gay people and wish they didn't exist, right?" If someone believes that teachers should do more to support students, someone could come along and make a strawman argument, disagreeing because, "I don't think students should be spoon fed."

Understandably, this kind of fallacy not only muddies the waters, but it very quickly leads to arguments, as nobody wants to be mischaracterized or dealt with on terms they haven't actually agreed to. There are some specific ways in which people tend to construct strawman's out of other people's arguments. Oversimplifying, generalizing and exaggerating the opponent's arguments is among the most common ways to do this, but it's not the only one. Sometimes, the other person will focus on specific parts of your argument while ignoring the others. Obviously, these tend to be the unflattering parts of the argument. Another way people construct strawmen is to deploy fringe or extreme points generally used either alongside the opponent's argument or to support it but which the opponent himself did not deploy. So, if someone claims that a fetus is a baby, one might strawman it by saying that they want to control women's bodies or prevent them from exercising their autonomy when in fact the person might only have been trying to make a biological argument.

A great way to make sure students don't fall into the temptation of battling against strawmen instead of real arguments, is to encourage them to debate, either amongst themselves or with you. Setting up a strawman is often a combination of a few things: a genuine lack of comprehension of the argument, a lack of empathy and understanding, and a desire to win and be righteous that is stronger than the desire to engage meaningfully with the material.

Consistently draw your student's attention to the difference between fact and opinion. Encourage them to zoom in on the bare bones of the argument, rather than getting carried away with narratives, colorful details or judgments. The goal is not only to truly understand what your opponent is saying, but to have the maturity and respect to engage with that view directly and in earnest.

It's also a good practice to give your opponent the benefit of doubt. This can be done by taking them at their best-case scenario. Let's say someone argues that America should become a communist country because this would promote greater equality. Take them at their best by assuming that what they're saying is true even if it isn't, and then go on to point holes in their argument. For example, you might say that freedom of religion will be impacted or that the state might come to exercise overarching control over our lives. Once you've attacked their best-case scenario effectively, you can then attack the things you previously assumed to be true to show that in reality the implications of the argument are far worse.

Here, a teacher who can model a growth mindset will find it natural to encourage students away from ego-based argument (i.e. doing whatever it takes to "win" and demonstrate superiority) and towards argument that is based on curiosity, mutual respect and intellectual rigor. Remind them that if they have to strawman someone's argument to win, then they are missing the entire point of engaging in discussion in the first place. Ask your student to debate with another or argue their case, then be on the lookout for a strawman. One time-honored technique is to ask your student to argue their opponent's case instead of their own. This will more firmly put them in a different perspective and encourage them to consider the argument more seriously.

Perspective-based questions: "I've heard you say what their argument is, but how do you think *they* would describe their position? Do you think they would find your description of them accurate?"

Closed questions or factual questions: "Do you have any actual evidence for that claim?" or, "Can you identify the actual claim being made here?"

Deepening or expanding questions: "What are your own biases here and how do you think they influence your position?"

False Dilemma Fallacy

Now let's look at a fallacy that is sadly encouraged and exacerbated by conventional education. Think of multiple choice questions, where the answer is only one of a handful of questions, or where the student is asked to say whether a statement is true or false. While these are useful, they can unwittingly train us to believe that the realm of knowledge is far more black and white than it probably is.

Since time immemorial, teachers have been asking students to respond to choices that are forced, artificial or unnatural. Though we necessarily have to simplify the world in our teaching models, what we don't want to do is teach our students to think in all-or-nothing ways, assuming that if something isn't right, it's wrong, and that there's no grey area in between.

A false dichotomy is best exemplified by (yet again) the famous politician's statement that "you are either with us or against us." Of course, this completely obscures the fact that you can occupy some third space in between, where maybe you agree only somewhat, or else you understand the issue in such a way that the framing of the situation doesn't make any sense for you.

False dilemmas incorrectly narrow the range of options that exist in reality. This is usually done to force someone to behave in a certain way or agree to something they might not otherwise. But it isn't always manipulative—sometimes we ourselves can make an error in the very first step of a problem when we falsely assume we only have two options. A dichotomous question (i.e. a yes/no question) can be appropriate at times, but is best used when there really are only two options ("Did this man die in 1976 or didn't he?").

This fallacy can be somewhat hard to counter because it feeds into a common cognitive distortion we suffer from known as "black-and-white thinking." In this distortion, you come to believe that there are only two outcomes in a given situation, one which is very positive and another that is very negative. This is why politicians are often seen exploiting the false dilemma fallacy. It's a powerful rhetorical device that does work with many people. We might even use the false dilemma fallacy in our own lives, like when we think that if we don't lose weight, nobody will consider us attractive. In cases like this, you see both the fallacy and the cognitive distortion working together because they often go hand in hand.

The best way to show your student the ridiculousness of false-dilemmas is to put them in one! Lived experience is powerful. If you tell them, "There are only two kinds of people in the world, those who love my algebra classes, and idiots," then they will quickly understand the problem. It also helps to try and note whether the person making the false dilemma is trying to get you to do something that benefits them. In such a scenario, think about whether making the decision they want you to is genuinely in your best interests. If it's not, calling them out on their manipulation is the best way to deal with the situation. However, false dichotomies in real life are a lot harder to identify and have always been a powerful way to manipulate people.

"You can't leave me, because then you'll be alone and you'll be miserable."

"We have to act right now and retaliate or we'll miss our opportunity completely."

"Either you eat loads of sugar and become obese and diabetic, or you abstain and live a healthy life."

To bring student's attention to false dichotomies, whether in their own arguments or in the material they encounter (including from you!) ask them a few pointed questions:

Critique or evaluative questions: "Do you think that claim is sound? Is that really true?"

Rhetorical questions: "What if there was a third option? What if it's not A or B but C? Or none of them?"

Deductive questions or loaded questions: "So, if the only option is to eat loads of sugar or none at all, then does that mean there are no people who eat a moderate amount of sugar?"

Circular Argument Fallacies or Begging the Question

Again, here is a logical fallacy that many students in fact learn from teachers and parents. A classic example is:

"Don't smoke pot, it's bad."
"Why is it bad?"
"Because it's illegal."
"But why is it illegal?"
"Because it's bad, that's why!"

A circular argument only *looks* like an argument—it's actually not one at all, but simply a restatement of the original claim. It's like saying: "Pot is bad because pot is bad." Not very convincing, and not a great way to gain sophisticated knowledge about the world! Sure, circular arguments typically pose the same claim in very different terms, so that it appears that you are being offered an explanation. But it takes real skill to notice when something isn't an explanation or a cause, but simply a repetition. In other words, the conclusion is somewhere along the line also presented as a premise for that same conclusion.

"My mom says pot is bad, and she's always right. I know this because she told me herself."

"Everyone loves chocolate flavor because chocolate is the most popular flavor."

"This movie is a masterpiece because it's very well made."

"You have to take your vitamins every day because daily vitamins are necessary."

Circular arguments can often appear in much more complex forms that are harder to notice and counter. This is especially true of scholarly work. The basic feature of every circular argument is that it already presupposes the thing that it is trying to prove. To be clear, this isn't logically incorrect. If the premises, or what an argument is based on, is true, then it follows that the conclusion must be correct as well. A common but often hard to debunk way in which this fallacy manifests is through arguments about God. People claim Jesus exists because the New Testament says so, and they also claim that the New Testament says so because Jesus did in fact exist. This argument is of the form "A is true because B is true, and B is true because A is true." To defeat such an argument, simply pointing out the circular nature of the argument isn't enough, because like we've noted, the argument is actually logically sound. As such, we must fall back on the Socratic method to make our interlocutor talk more about their argument and expose cracks in them.

As you've probably noticed, many of these fallacies are slippery things, and often come combined with other fallacies. Sometimes, you'll have to sit with your student and carefully pick through an argument, trying first to understand what you're looking at before you can begin the work of appraising it. But using questions this way not only focuses your student's mind, but models for them an attitude of open-mindedness and curiosity. Show them that they shouldn't blindly accept any one position until they've actually thought it through.

The way to help your students understand this fallacy and work around it, is to simply keep challenging them to provide real evidence. A circular argument isn't an argument—so keep asking your students to actually make an argument. Here, you can take the approach of any two year old and keep asking, "Why?" to whatever claim they make. Eventually, they will notice themselves saying the same thing over and over again!

Cause-and-effect questions: "So what exactly makes chocolate the best flavor?"

Evaluative questions: "Can you clearly outline your evidence? What proof do you have?"

Analytical questions: "Could you write your argument out for me, step by step?" or, "Has this person actually given a reason for their opinion or simply restated their opinion?"

Causal Fallacies

A final group of fallacies we'll consider concerns cause and effect, and these can be surprisingly difficult to catch in real life. Causal fallacies can come in all shapes and sizes, but they're always about arriving at unproven conclusions. As an example, you could arrive at a conclusion when the evidence isn't sufficient to do so: "You live on the coastline so you probably love being in the water." It might be true, but if the only evidence you have is that they live near the water, it's not quite enough.

The *post hoc ergo propter hoc* fallacy basically means the fallacy of assuming that if B came after A, then A must have caused B. "She's been drinking nettle tea for a month and her cancer has gone into remission, so nettle must have some anti-cancer properties," or, "I was wearing these underpants when I got promoted, so these are now my lucky underpants!"

Superstitions, dumb luck, wishful thinking, and other flimsy explanations for why things happen as they do obviously need to be closely examined. This is, after all, why the scientific method exists—so that we can tease out causal relationships properly and make meaningful claims about how certain events and phenomena unfold around us.

Another variation is called *cum hoc ergo propter hoc*, which refers to the mistaken assumption that two things happening together must necessarily be related. An example is, "People who drink wheatgrass juice also appear to live longer than everyone else. It must be that wheatgrass juice increases your longevity!" What this fallacy misses is a little like what black-and-white thinking misses—there could be another explanation. There may be a third variable, as yet unseen, causing both observed facts. In our example, being wealthy might be associated both with better longevity (because of better health care) and with the consumption of wheatgrass juice. Again, the scientific method is what helps us identify these "confounding variables" so that we can accurately locate the source of a cause.

This fallacy is also called "correlation doesn't imply causation" and is a very important concept for all students to grasp. If you catch your student making this error, use it as a teaching opportunity. Have them literally write down the premises of their argument and the conclusion they're drawing from it. Ask them if the premises genuinely do lead to the conclusion. To help them think it through, offer alternative explanations for the same conclusion. Or, you could give them a more obvious example and ask them to spot the error.

For example, say the following: "There are a lot of doctors in this town, and also a very high rate of cancer. Therefore, the doctors must somehow be causing all the cancer!" Ask them to explain exactly *why* this argument is so silly. If you can get them to spell it out to you for themselves, they'll more easily notice when they make a similar error. Another example is: "The number of shark attacks seems to rise in proportion to the amount of ice cream people eat. I guess that means that eating ice cream causes people to get attacked by sharks more." For this last example, you could try to lead the student to hidden variables, i.e. the fact that summer causes both an increase in ice cream consumption and more people swimming in the ocean!

Analytical questions: "Can you identify the evidence you're giving? Can you show *how* your evidence supports your claim? If someone else made this argument, would you think it was a good one?"

Metacognition questions: "Now that you know about this fallacy, can you think of any examples yourself? Can you identify it in your own work?"

Critique and defend questions: "You say XYZ. Do you have proof? How do you respond to my claim that XYZ is actually false?"

We've spent a lot of time in this chapter exploring cognitive fallacies not because our students are studying philosophy or formal logic, but because solid critical thinking skills are a part of *any* student's learning journey. With a good familiarity of all the ways our thinking can go astray, we can guard against it in ourselves and learn to recognize it in our students.

By using questions, we can guide or students to recognize their own errors. The overarching skill is that the student gets comfortable looking at their own thoughts and arguments and learns to hold their own cognition to a higher standard. It's hard to think of any learning endeavor, at any level, that isn't improved when a student gains this ability.

Takeaways

- No matter your subject, your lesson plan, or the age and stage of your student, you can draw on several time-tested educational principles.
- The Goldilocks principle is very intuitive: we should pitch the difficulty of our lessons "just right"—where they won't be too difficult nor too easy; some researchers have found this golden middle zone at the place the student has eighty-five percent success with the task. This theory is related to the Yerkes-Dodson law, which describes a non-linear relationship between arousal and performance. Our job as teachers is to know our students and adjust difficulty so they are always optimally challenged but not overwhelmed.
- It can be difficult to truly know when a student understands something, so we

have to use questions and infer from their answers their level of understanding. Heick's taxonomy is a list of isolated tasks that increase in complexity. If your student can complete these tasks, you can assume they possess understanding at that level.

- There are six domains to tests understanding: the parts, the whole, interconnectedness, the function, the abstraction, and the self. You can test understanding using activities or direct questions, although not all tasks require understanding at all six levels.

- Clear communication is obviously essential. A lot depends on your ability to explain concepts to your students. The first step is to give a clear and delineated definition of the concept, and then to carefully use analogies, examples, elaborations, and metaphors to guide your student towards understanding.

- A teacher needs to be on guard for logical fallacies in their students in their quest to help them cultivate better critical thinking skills. By using pointed questions (i.e. the Socratic method) teachers can draw attention to fallacies such as ad hominem, straw man, false dilemma, and causal errors. Questions can be of many different kinds and can encourage students' self-awareness, reflection, and metacognition.

Chapter 3. Visible Learning

Earlier in this book, we saw how important it was to abandon our assumptions about teaching and focus only on those techniques and methods that have hard evidence to support their effectiveness. So, in this chapter, having considered different pedagogical approaches, basic teaching principles and the teacher mindset best associated with learning, let's return to John Hattie and his research into what really helps students learn. In this way, he attempted to make learning "visible" i.e. transparent and evidence-based with no mystery.

Synthesizing 1200 metanalyses on the factors that affect teaching outcomes, Hattie looked at six areas, including the student, the school, the curriculum, the teacher, and the learning approach taken. As a teacher, you have control over only some of these aspects, and you're most interested in the latter—the teaching methods.

Overall, there are 138 influences on learning, each with different "effect sizes." Some influences actually have a *negative* effect on learning. Before we see what works, let's take a brief look at what definitely doesn't. The biggest impediment to student learning by far is the presence of ADHD and deafness, for understandable reasons. Things like boredom and depression also significantly undermine learning, as does lack of sleep.

Though you likely don't have control over them, it's worth being aware of some home and life factors that might be handicapping your student, such as frequently moving schools, being held back a grade, being expelled or excluded, having parents that are on military deployment, or being on welfare. Corporal punishment is negatively associated with learning, and things like high TV use or the "vacation effect" are also impediments.

You might be surprised to find that a range of your favorite teaching tools and techniques have no or minimal effect on learning, such as using humor, open plan classrooms, better technology for distance learning, single-sex schools, extracurricular activities, mindfulness, or (to many students' vindication) homework.

So, what does work?

At the very top of the list, with the highest effect size of 1.57, was what is called "collective teacher efficacy." To put this into perspective, this factor is considered to be *more than twice as effective* as something like, say, feedback, which has an effect size of just 0.70. Collective teacher efficacy is about how teachers, as a whole, feel about their competency when it comes to teaching. This is a tricky factor because it's not about individual confidence levels, but rather a shared understanding of teachers' power to meaningfully help their students.

In a way, Hattie is attempting to make teacher's feel better about their effectiveness by arming them with proven techniques, so they *know* it is possible to have an impact. This confidence, unsurprisingly, comes through in their teaching, and students benefit from this sense of security more than anything else their teachers focus on. Though this is a rich and worthwhile topic to investigate, we will move on and consider only the best *practical* teaching approaches that we can realistically apply for ourselves.

Trust Students to Self-Grade

With an effect size of 1.44, the next on our list of interest in called "self-reported grades." Hattie found that using this technique advanced student achievement by around three years—which is mind blowing, to say the least. To understand self-reported grades, let's use an example. I could tell a student to tackle a series of math problems. Then, I could grade them and find all the things they did wrong, and give them a grade that essentially says,

"This wasn't good enough." This is more or less how traditional grading works.

With self-reported grading, however, you ask *your student* to set their own goal for their performance, which is phrased as a kind of prediction. This turns the process on its head. So, before doing the math test, you have a discussion with your student. What are their goals? How confident are they feeling about their future performance? Once they've set a goal/prediction for themselves, then you as a teacher can give them the guidance and support they need to reach it.

This simple technique is enough to make students perform better, as shown by plenty of research assessed by Hattie. Let's be honest, teachers usually hate grading and students don't particularly like getting work back with a big grade stamped on the front, either. So why not try something different? You could see yourself not as a *giver* of grades, but rather as facilitator or fact checker of your student's own assessments. How well are they really doing? There's no reason that this information should be obvious to you but hidden from them.

So, perhaps what works about his approach is that the student is engaged meaningfully and becomes part of their own learning process, rather than just receiving a static grade externally. You may be surprised with just how accurate your students grades really are—and don't we want to encourage more self-awareness and reflection?

There are many ways to use this in your lessons or classes. One popular way is peer-grading. Have students grade one another according to a mutually agreed upon rubric. They will simultaneously understand and identify learning goals, as well as reflexively understand how their progress fits comparatively with their peers. The whole process has a sort of self-correcting power—students can often be more tuned into the fine points of their work than you'd expect. Take some time to devise a marking strategy together, then assign them one or more projects to grade accordingly. Their final score is the average of their peer marker's scores. This process can make students feel confident and capable in themselves, and they are often more than willing to be fair. You can use the marking process itself to drive further lessons.

The classic way of having student self-report grades is to create a form or template and encourage your student to complete it according to how they appraise their progress. These can be found online or made from scratch according to your needs. Use a personal grade tracker to help your student take responsibility for their own learning. It can be wonderful for a student to know that you are not standing off to the side, judging their performance, being mean, and looking for all the things they're doing wrong. Rather, you're there to encourage their own natural learning—and part of that is understanding where they are on their learning path.

Ask your student regularly:

- How do you think you did on that exercise?

- What would you like to achieve on this next project?
- How would you rate your progress?
- What score would you give yourself when it comes to this skill?
- How can we improve that score together?

Use the Power of Metacognition

Let's move on. The next most impactful influence, at 1.29, are jointly "teacher estimates of achievement" and "cognitive task analysis." The former basically refers to expectations that teachers have of their student's performance, and the latter is about encouraging students to think about their thinking, and the cognitive tasks they perform in any learning activity (i.e. a focus on the cognitive tools of a task rather than just its outcome).

By now, most people know that teacher expectations can have a powerful effect on student performance. Sadly, if a teacher has bias and prejudice against a student, this can translate to lower expectations of what they're capable of. Unsurprisingly, students respond to this, and these low expectations become a kind of self-fulfilling prophesy. It works the other way round, too: when teachers have faith and belief in a student, they inevitably perform to fulfil those high expectations.

Let's focus on the more practical influence, however—the cognitive task analysis. To understand what Hattie means by this, we need only understand that as teachers, we are always teaching simultaneously at two levels: we are teaching about the specific content or information in a specific lesson, and we are also teaching about how to learn. What Hattie found was that lessons that focus on the second style of teaching tend to be more effective for students.

What does cognitive task analysis look like?

There is a difference between skills and knowledge. As students learn, they perform all kinds of cognitive tasks, such as problem solving, memory, critical thinking, attention, and so on. In cognitive task analysis, students are encouraged to be aware of these cognitive tasks they are performing. In doing so, they can take charge and use these higher-order skills to solve problems more effectively. In essence, you are teaching them the skill of thinking about any data, rather than just bits and pieces of specific data.

It sounds a little complicated but makes a lot of sense when applied in lessons. And it makes your life easier, too! You want to use a reflective and integrative approach and gently draw your student's attention to the bigger picture. Just as we did in the section on logical fallacies, this approach has us encouraging students to be aware not of *what* they are thinking, but *how* they are thinking about it.

Don't be afraid to use language that describes exactly what you're doing. A great technique is to solve problems and questions with your student by asking them to highlight task or instruction words that alert them to the kind of thinking they'll do: "compare and contrast," "explain," "define," "solve," etc. Ask your student to tell you explicitly what this means and what they have to do.

"The question says solve so I will have to use my problem solving skills."
"And what problem solving skills do we have when it comes to this kind of problem?"
"Well, I could try writing down what I already know on this side, and write down the thing I'm supposed to find on the other side..."

This way, your student is working at the level of their own cognition, and not just at the level of the problem solving. They are using metacognition (as well as first-order cognition) and this is the start of them being able to self-reflect and adjust as they go, eventually without your help. Constantly encourage discussion about the learning process:

"What did you try and did your approach work?"
"Can you tell me what cognitive skills you feel you practiced in today's lesson?"

"Out of the skills we need to work this problem, which are you strongest at, and which need more practice?"

Teachers often find it useful to make little icons, symbols or images to quickly convey abstract concepts. Once students are familiar with the tasks of, for example, critical thinking, memory and creative writing, you can use a visual shorthand in your teaching materials, like a little cartoon brain, a memory card, and a pencil. This can make your students more comfortable and familiar with using and discussing abstract cognitive principles with you.

Tackle the Big Problems First

With an effect size of around 1.29 (the same as "teacher estimates of achievement" and "cognitive task analysis") *response to intervention* basically means that you give targeted help to those children in a classroom who are struggling. The idea is to get in there early to identify those students who are not managing well, give them what they need as soon as possible, and then regularly monitor and reassess them as you go. In previous versions of his research, Hattie had "interventions for students with learning disabilities" as an influence, too.

Given that Hattie also found that the presence of ADHD or deafness was one of the most *negative* influences on student success, it makes sense that having an approach that reverses or corrects this disadvantage is going to have the biggest quantifiable effect, if you get it right. At this point, you might be wondering how this would apply to you if you are teaching only a few children, or even just one, and exactly how you could apply this approach if your student doesn't have any disability or difficulty.

Hattie believed that *all* children could benefit from an approach that is targeted and tailored to them as individuals. Nevertheless, just because this influence has been easy for Hattie and his researchers to observe and analyze from a research perspective, it doesn't mean he can provide any insight on what to do with these observations. Hattie discovered that early intervention and regular monitoring of struggling students helped a lot—but his job as a researcher wasn't to tell teachers *which* early interventions to use or how to monitor their effects.

For that, unfortunately, the teacher is still largely responsible. It can be tricky to give advice on how to operationalize this idea in the classroom. An easy way to implement the general idea, however, is to use the principle of "lowest hanging fruit" in your teaching. Think about someone who is trying to lose weight. If they are extremely overweight and have hundreds of pounds to lose, then they could eat amounts that would seem enormous to others and still lose weight so long as they are eating less relative to what they normally do. On the other hand, someone who is already at a healthy weight or even underweight may find it a lot harder to lose one or two pounds.

This principle applies to many areas of life—when you are a beginner or have a long way to go, the early parts of the learning curve often bring the biggest gains, which taper off as you improve. Thinking of it this way, it's no surprise that Hattie found that the biggest gains were made by students who were struggling. In the same way that a very overweight person can lose astonishing amounts of weight, a student who is struggling simply has greater opportunity for improvement.

All of this is to say that as a teacher, your most effective strategy may be to make those large and easy gains first, i.e. start with the low hanging fruit. Ways you can do this:

- Avoid focusing on what your student is already doing easily (since only minimal gains can be made there) and instead pick the area that is most challenging. Though it may seem more challenging at first, your student will derive greater satisfaction and make bigger strides, which will improve their confidence.
- If you have multiple students with mixed abilities, get the more advanced students to explain to and teach the struggling students.

- Frequently test improvements at every lesson.
- Begin each lesson with the most challenging aspect, when attention and energy are highest. The psychological feeling of achievement will allow you to end on a positive note with some reflection on what's been achieved.

Pitch Lessons at the Right Level

At an effect size of around 1.28 the next biggest influence on student achievement is not so much a single technique, but a broad approach to teaching inspired by developmental psychologist Jean Piaget. The idea is that if you understand the developmental stage your student is at, then you can match your teaching and assessment strategies to fit them most appropriately.

This is not rocket science, but unfortunately it is something that teachers can overlook when getting carried away with curricula and specific techniques. What Hattie's research seems to suggest is that it's not the lesson or teaching strategy per se, but rather how well it suits the student and fits where they are in their learning path. In other words, it's a question of timing—a lesson that would be inspiring and illuminating for a student at age thirteen could be incredibly challenging and overwhelming for them at age eleven. As a teacher, your job is to make sure your student is getting the lesson they most need at the right time.

Though there isn't enough space to explore all the details of Piaget's theory (although interested teachers should definitely read further on his ideas), we can quickly overview the main stages. Each stage is an achievement in a student's journey to more complex, abstract thought and away from concrete and sensory processing. The first is the **sensorimotor stage**, from birth to two years old. You're unlikely to be teaching a child this young, so we'll skip over this stage, but suffice to say that it involves concrete, sensation-based learning rather than abstract concepts.

The **preoperational stage** is from two to seven years old, and children here are heavily engaged in imaginary play. As a teacher, you can take advantage of this stage of development by presenting activities in terms of pretending games and play, rather than directly abstract notions. So, spelling can be taught by telling stories about the shape that each letter makes, and counting with stories about fish eating coins, for example, rather than just abstract letters and numbers.

The **concrete operational stage** is from age seven to eleven. Here, abstract thought is beginning to develop, but not yet fully. Your teaching should still be in the concrete realm, however, i.e. doing sums on fingers or an abacus rather than in the head. Your goal is to always tie concepts to the real world somehow, such as with pictures, stories, or actual objects.

The **formal operational stage** is from eleven years onwards, and is the time when students can be expected to practice abstract thinking or self-reflection. The metacognition tasks discussed earlier will be manageable for them, and they are able to think about thinking, and manipulate ideas and concepts more easily. But you'll notice there's a big age range. Ideally, you would start with more concrete tasks and gradually introduce more abstract elements as the student was ready. For example, you could read a written story and answer comprehension questions, but then open it up to the student and ask them to conjure up alternative endings or entirely new stories.

You don't need to be an educational psychologist to understand where your student is developmentally. You can get a feel for this by making sure they have a good mix of easy tasks and challenges, and observing how they respond. Remember, too, that every student is different, and their pace of development is unique. The Piagetian approach helps us understand that the best material for our student is the material that fits their level, wherever they are.

Get Students to Connect

The final influence we'll look at is the Jigsaw method, with an effect rating of 1.20. After this, the effect ratings drop off sharply—it's not that they aren't effective, it's just that the five or so that we're considering here are the *most* effective. This method was actually first devised as a way to defuse tense classroom environments, but was later used primarily for its educational value. We have encountered jigsaw exercises earlier in the book, and saw how teachers can assign students only a piece of a task and encourage them to collaborate to meet the task's ends. This is a classic integrative and collaborative approach— and Hattie found that it really worked.

The approach is best suited for groups of students. To make it effective, start by setting a clear goal that the entire group has to achieve. Then, distribute the task amongst the students. They could each be given a paragraph of a text, or a different question to answer, or a different set of facts (i.e. different pieces of the jigsaw). Next, outline the terms of interaction between the students—give them a time limit, for example, or ask them to move around and chat in pairs.

Finally, you can end with students individually synthesizing what they've gathered, or else compile a response to the main objective as a group. As a teacher you can use prompts to guide students, and remind them of their goal. How you arrange the jigsaw activity is up to you, but aim to have the three stages:

- Setting objectives and parameters
- Allowing students to interact to solve the problem together
- Synthesizing what's learned, either individually or in a group

Jigsaws work because students are encouraged to develop real, applied knowledge of a task when they communicate what they know and learn what other students know. Comprehension and memory improve—not to mention students typically enjoy these exercises and can simultaneously develop better communication and empathy! Start with small jigsaw activities to start (you could literally cut an information sheet into pieces for younger students and have them reassemble it) and adjust according to what works for your group. You could combine the final synthesizing stage with a chance for some reflection and metacognition.

Visible learning can be a bit tricky to get your head around at first, since the approaches that have the most scientific evidence are often not those that are conventionally emphasized. Many teachers are looking for a quick gimmick or trick that will make things easier for themselves and their students, but the surprise is that what most works often has nothing to do with the technique used.

Luckily, what Hattie's research shows us is that you don't need mountains of clever activities and techniques to be a good teacher. Instead, you can be confident that if you apply some of the aspects discussed in this chapter, you can't help but improve student outcomes. Involve your students in their learning process, get them to think about their thinking, tackle the big challenges first, and make sure that lessons fit your student's developmental stage. And if you have a group, then you can't beat jigsaw activities for effectiveness.

Takeaways

- Educational researcher John Hattie synthesized 1200 teaching studies to form a meta-study examining the influence of different aspects on student learning outcomes. He ranked around 138 according to their effect, and believed that good teachers should commit to evidence-based approaches.
- Surprisingly, the biggest influence on student learning has to do with teacher attitudes: when teachers collectively believe in their efficacy as teachers, students benefit.
- Students benefit when they can self-grade, rather than being graded externally by a teacher. This allows students to take responsibility and ownership over their learning and develop self-awareness and insight. They're also usually quite accurate!

- Metacognition has great effects on student outcomes. Teachers can encourage students to think about their thinking and self-reflect on the cognitive tasks they are performing, over and above the content of the task.
- Tackling student difficulties directly can have the biggest effect on outcomes, i.e. teachers should work closely with struggling students or those with learning disabilities. They can do this by intervening as soon as possible and assessing the effect of that intervention regularly.
- Teachers are likely to have more success if they pitch their lessons at the right developmental level. Students differ in their formal operational cognitive ability, i.e. the capacity for abstract thought. Teachers can adjust levels of abstraction and observe their students, so their lessons respect their developmental stage.
- Finally, students seem to learn best with jigsaw-style exercises that encourage group cooperation, interaction and communication. The teacher can

combine this with self-reflection and metacognition to anchor and summarize the lesson at the end.

Chapter 4. Student Mindset

Teachers can often have difficulty not with the material itself or finding the smartest, most efficient way to present it—rather, their trouble comes in when they try to inspire and motivate students who simply don't care! It's as though in teaching, there are always two lessons running in parallel—one concerning the actual material at hand, and another running in the background, where the student is learning discipline, stamina and self-regulation as they move through the process of learning.

Academic Buoyancy

The concept of *academic buoyancy* is the second key to overcoming our own internal obstacles to learning.

Learning is bound to be difficult, even for those with supposed innate intelligence. Nothing comes easy, at least not at the levels of mastery we are aiming for. And yet, so many people take themselves out of the running by giving up at the first sign of hardship.

People who *don't* give up when they're faced with learning challenges are said to have *academic buoyancy*. Like intelligence, this isn't an inborn characteristic that some are born with, but rather a set of skills that can be learned and habits that can be cultivated to result in the ability to push past challenges and keep learning.

Confidence is just one element of academic buoyancy, but confidence alone is what allows us to overcome our fears and anxieties. In the first chapter, we discussed how confidence can unlock your lack of motivation. Imagine how much more empowered you would feel with the hardships of learning if you could embody every element.

Researchers from the University of Sydney and the University of Oxford have identified five Cs that, if developed, will result in academic buoyancy. These five Cs are *composure, confidence, coordination, commitment, and control.* They are not specific to learning, but they are traits that certainly improve it.

It will be apparent why these qualities are important to overcoming obstacles associated with learning—most of them are truly not about the content or information itself. Rather, most obstacles have to do with our mindset; our belief and sense of perseverance ends up being what separates most effective learners at the end of the day. Their influence is far, far greater than any of the techniques in this book. Is this to say that where there is a will, there is a way? Yes—learning in large part depends on how you feel about it, and the rest is just about saving time and working smarter.

Composure is the ability to manage and minimize anxiety. When learners feel anxious while engaging in their studies, it's usually because they're afraid of being ashamed and embarrassed. What if people find out we're trying to learn something, and expect us to display our knowledge? What if we fail completely when this happens? *What if we fail?* The fear can be paralyzing.

When people can't manage their anxiety, they are weighed down by their fear and crippled by the tension it produces in their bodies. In the worst cases, worries overcome the thoughts of the learner, preventing the student from focusing on and understanding new information. But there's good news: those fears are entirely baseless.

As anxiety is largely based on the fear of failure, we must directly address that. When we think about fear, we think about the worst-case scenario. Whatever we "fail" at, we imagine the world ending as a direct result. This is known as catastrophization, and it occurs whenever you ignore the realistic consequences and jump to drastic conclusions.

This tendency is conquered by managing your self-talk. Acknowledge that negative things may happen, but that many of your thoughts may be irrational and fictitious. Consider the alternative explanations and outcomes.

If you find yourself worrying, counter that worry with optimism. If you berate yourself for a mistake, remind yourself that it's a learning opportunity and that you'll do better next time. Any negative thought can be successfully and honestly countered by positive, encouraging, forgiving, and accepting alternatives. With time, the brain comes to accept these retorts as more valid than the negative, fearful thoughts. If anxiety is a problem for you, be persistent. This bugaboo really can be beaten. You can gain the composure you need to be academically buoyant.

Confidence, also called self-efficacy, is the belief that you are able to perform a specific task. When we lack confidence, we are

157

certain we can't successfully accomplish a goal. We talk ourselves down, insult ourselves, and belittle any progress we make. When this happens, we often give up on our goal early before we can prove to ourselves and others that we're a failure. The trouble is that giving up is failing too; it can be satisfying to confirm these negative beliefs about ourselves, but it's far more satisfying—and less stressful—to set our doubts aside and actually reach our goals.

If you're ready to improve your confidence, there are two main techniques to employ. The first, as we saw in the section on composure, is self-talk. When your brain tells you that you're a failure or that a subject is too hard for you to learn, counter that thought with an assertion that you're going to keep studying, and with time and effort, you will succeed. If you keep questioning these thoughts, they really will fade in time.

The second method is more concrete: goal-setting. We gain confidence naturally when we accomplish tasks. When we have a track record of success, it becomes harder and harder to believe our doubts have any credibility. The fastest way to do this is to create daily, or even hourly, study goals, and to watch yourself meet them over and over again. When this happens, congratulate yourself! Each goal you reach gets you one step closer to your ultimate goal of skill mastery. More than that, each goal you reach demonstrates that you have the skill and fortitude to reach the targets you set for yourself. It's a sign that your confidence is real and legitimate.

Coordination is your ability to plan and manage your time effectively. When people fail to do this, they often fall prey to *The Planning Fallacy*. This fallacy points out that people are poor at determining how long tasks take to complete. As a general rule, we presume tasks will take less time than they actually need. Worse, when we presume things won't take very long, we often put those tasks off, because we feel like we have plenty of time to get them done. This is usually untrue, and then we find ourselves with late assignments and failed work tasks.

Several steps can be taken to eliminate this problem. Minimizing distractions in your work area is a great way to start. Turn off your phone, close your door, and tell friends or family that you're busy and not to be disturbed. You should invariably do this soon after you gain a new task to complete or subject to study. Putting things off leads to being late, while doing them immediately takes advantage of all the time you have. Lastly, it's best to do the longest, most difficult task first. Leaving it for last will produce a false sense of security and may lead to your work being incomplete at the time it's due. Getting it out of the way does the opposite, setting you up for easier tasks and an early finish.

Commitment, also called grit, is a combination of passion and persistence that can be nurtured to help you reach your goals. It's easy to study for a day or a week, but attempts to build new habits often fail. We find ourselves listlessly settling into the couch to watch another movie or television show, without putting any more effort into bettering ourselves. This keeps us in the same life situation, wasting precious time, when we could be using those same hours to improve ourselves and our circumstances.

As in the previous two categories, self-talk can be a useful tool in bolstering commitment. Talking yourself into doing things and ensuring yourself that you can make it to the end are useful tools. Having others support you in a similar way and encourage you to study when you're flagging can bolster your sense of personal responsibility and keep you trucking along even when your energy is waning.

Finally, understanding what you are sacrificing and committing for can be powerful. Without a sense of how we stand to benefit, or what pain we will clearly avoid, we can sometimes lose motivation. What dreams does this information help you attain? What hardships and difficulties will be removed once you master this information? Keep these in mind and know that you are working for something greater than the current moment of discomfort.

Finally, **control**. We have to feel like we can control our fates. There are multiple aspects of this. First, we should feel that we have the ability and capacity to achieve the learning outcomes we want. Lacking this makes us feel like we are in motion just for motion's sake, never getting closer to the end goal. We covered this in an earlier chapter, but there is no real thing as innate intelligence. Well, there is, but it doesn't really affect ninety-nine percent of us in the middle of the bell curve. Understand that with hard work, the result you want is possible, and that struggles are an unavoidable part of the process. Discomfort should be the expectation, not the exception.

Second, we should feel a sense of ownership over our learning process. When we have a sense of control in our work, we feel personal responsibility, or a sense of ownership, that propels us to do our best and keep working in the face of setbacks. When we don't have that, working and studying can seem futile, like a waste of time. We will simply feel that we are being told what to do, and this is adding insult to injury.

This can be addressed by proactively making sure of what your goals are and tailoring your everyday work to reach them. Take your fate into your own hands and create your own plan. You always have the choice to float toward other people's expectations, goals, and plans, or create a personalized set for yourself to follow.

Learning in itself is not a difficult task. But missing any of these academic buoyancy elements will simply set you up for failure. They are more prerequisites to effective learning than tactics in themselves.

Academic buoyancy is perhaps better framed as *resilience*: the ability to adapt to stressful situations. More resilient people are able to "roll with the punches" and adapt to adversity without lasting difficulties; less resilient people have a harder time with stress and life changes, both major and minor. It's been found that those who deal with minor stresses more easily can also manage major crises with greater ease, so resilience has its benefits for daily life as well as for the rare major catastrophe.

Psychologist Susan Kobasa noted three elements to resilience: (1) looking at difficulties as a challenge, (2) committing to achieving a goal no matter what, and (3) limiting their efforts and even concerns only to factors that they have control over.

Another psychologist named Martin Seligman noted three different elements of resilience: (1) seeing negative events as temporary and limited, (2) not letting negative events define them or their perspective, and (3) not overly blaming or denigrating themselves for negative events. His general theme appears to be letting negativity pass as temporary and not indicative of personal shortcomings.

It's clear how any of those six resilience factors can play a role in achieving the learning goals we want. It's simply about how you bounce back from failure. Failure is a part of life, and it's what we do after the fact that determines our character and, ultimately, our success.

Productive Failure

In most situations, we tie accomplishment with success: winning, positive outcomes, and finding solutions. But in learning, a key component in achievement is *failing*.

Productive failure is an idea identified by Manu Kapur, a researcher at the National Institute of Education in Singapore. The philosophy builds on the learning paradox, wherein *not* arriving at the desired effect is as valuable as prevailing, if not more. This is not the emotional impact, but rather, the neurological impact.

Kapur stated that the accepted model of instilling knowledge—giving students structure and guidance early and continuing support until the students can get it on their own—might not be the best way to actually promote learning. Although that model intuitively makes sense, according to Kapur, it's best to let students flounder by themselves without outside help.

Kapur conducted a trial with two groups of students. In one group, students were given a set of problems with full instructional support from teachers on-site. The second group was given the same problems but received no teacher help whatsoever. Instead, the second group of students had to collaborate to find the solutions.

The supported group was able to solve the problems correctly, while the group left to itself was not. But without instructional support, this second group was forced to do deeper dives into the problems by working together. They generated ideas about the nature of the problems and speculated on what potential solutions might look like. They tried to understand the root of the problems and what methods were available to solve them. Multiple solutions, approaches, and angles were investigated that ended up providing a three-dimensional understanding of the problems.

The two groups were then tested on what they had just learned, and the results weren't even close. The group without teacher assistance *significantly outperformed* the other group. The group that did not solve the problems discovered what Kapur deemed a "hidden efficacy" in failure: they nurtured a deeper understanding of the structure of the problems through group investigation and process.

The second group may not have solved the problem itself, but they learned more about the aspects of the problem. Going forward, when those students encountered a new problem on another test, they were able to use the knowledge they generated through their trial more effectively than the passive recipients of an instructor's expertise.

Consequently, Kapur asserted that the important parts of the second group's process were their miscues, mistakes, and fumbling. When that group made the active effort to learn by themselves, they retained more knowledge needed for future problems.

Three conditions, Kapur said, make productive failure an effective process:

- Choose problems that "challenge but do not frustrate."

- Give learners the chance to explain and elaborate their processes.

- Allow learners to compare and contrast good and bad solutions.

Struggling with something is a positive condition to learning, though it requires discipline and a sense of delayed gratification. This runs counter to our instincts. How can we, so to speak, let failing work for us?

Chances are you'll come across a moment or two of defeat in your process, along with the temptation to give up. You may even sense this before you start, which can lead to crippling anxiety that can hover over your work.

Expect but don't succumb to frustration.

Anticipating frustration in advance is just good planning—but you also have to plan for how to deal with it. Sketch out a plan or idea on how to alleviate frustration when it happens—most often, this will be taking a break from the situation to recharge and getting some momentary distance from the problem. Quite often, the mere act of pausing allows for objectivity to seep in, letting you see the hang-up more clearly. But in any case, it will abate the most immediate anxieties you're feeling and give you the chance to approach the issue from a more relaxed frame of mind.

It's a matter of being comfortable with a state of mental discomfort and confusion. This can be akin to juggling ten balls in the air at once and not being sure when you can place them down.

Learning mode is different from results mode, and they have entirely different measures of success. When you want to learn, you are just looking for an increase in knowledge—*any* increase is successful learning. Reframe your expectations to make the learning as important as the result—*more* important, if possible.

Explicit and static knowledge, such as facts and dates, doesn't necessarily benefit from this. It doesn't need to. But transmitting deep and layered comprehension cannot just be plugged into the brain. It must be manipulated and applied, and failure is inherent in that process. In a way, failures function similarly to the types of questions we discussed in an earlier chapter, where they slowly allow you to triangulate knowledge and understanding based on what's *not* working and what's *not* true.

In the end, failure acts as a blueprint for our next steps. It is a test run that didn't go as planned and thus allows you to rectify pinpointed matters for the future.

For example, let's say you're planting a vegetable garden, noting the steps and techniques you use along the way, and when it's time to harvest, some of your plants don't come out the way they are supposed to. Is it because you used the wrong soil? Use your resources to find out *why* that soil was wrong and what it needs to look like. Was the failed plant too close to another? Learn techniques for maximizing placement within a small space.

Hidden in all of this is the fact that living and acting to avoid failure, even just in learning, leads to very different results than someone who actively seeks success. One approach wants to limit exposure and risk, while the other is focused on the end goal no matter the cost. Failure doesn't have to be your friend, but it *will* be your occasional companion, like it or not. With that in mind, it probably makes more sense to embody the approach that is about taking more risk—and also reaping greater rewards.

Freedom from Judgment

In a way, one of the best lessons any teacher can impart on any student is a healthy attitude toward risk and failure. The mindset with which we as teachers approach the entire learning process communicates powerfully to our students what the parameters of learning are, its values, and so on. And so if we talk about failure and how it can actually teach us more effectively than success, we also need to talk about the *psychological* aspects of failure when learning is concerned.

A learning environment free from judgment is one that fosters a robust attitude toward failure or defeat. If failure is so important to the learning process, we need to make sure our students feel free enough to take risks and try new things without feeling stupid for doing so. Judgment is an ego game—it's part of the "fixed mindset" that sees knowledge and learning as something to bolster one's personal identity, or win an argument.

The trouble is when the ego makes self-worth and identity dependent on success. The other side of this is that we then experience failure, mistakes, ignorance, delay or defeat as an attack to our very identity, and a threat to our self-worth. So, instead of thinking, "I failed," we think, "*I'm* a failure." You can see which attitude is most likely to lead to self-correction and learning. The irony is that clinging to the idea of being right and never making a mistake or failing makes us *less* resilient to adversity, and less likely to truly evolve and learn.

It's a paradox; when we embark on learning we obviously want to gain more mastery, insight and understanding. But the price for this is often the experience of being a beginner, who must constantly face their own ignorance and lack of skill. This is why it's important to appreciate the meta-skill of being able to tolerate not only failure, but uncertainty, ambiguity and complexity. A good teacher makes their student feel like they can experiment, try things, fail, adjust, and ask questions safely and without any consequences for their sense of self-worth or identity.

But you might be wondering—does learning really have to be such a grueling and mistake-ridden experience? Surely positive feelings of success and pride are also great motivators? You can imagine that routinely having to face your own shortcomings or defeats would quickly become demoralizing and lead to less learning, not more. To understand this balance better, we can turn to the concept of the Losada Ratio, first introduced by psychologists Marcial Losada and Barbara Frederickson.

The idea is that there is a fixed ratio of negative emotions to positive ones that would best support a successful, balanced life. Using mathematical models, the pair found the ideal ratio to fall between around three and eleven, meaning that the number of positive comments, ideas, thoughts, feelings etc. needed to be around three to eleven times greater than negative ones, in order for a person to thrive optimally.

Positive feedback, reward and reinforcement helps. But too much can have the opposite effect.

Criticism, failure and defat can also support learning. But too much can demotivate and frustrate. However, if people experience roughly three times as much positive information as negative, they will flourish. At ratios above 11:1, however, the performance gains are lost, i.e. the "Losada Line" is reached—at least according to this theory.

As it happens, the original Losada Ratio paper has now been seriously criticized for lacking scientific validity and the concept has been outright debunked. Nevertheless, its popularity does suggest that there is some value in the idea that positive and negative emotional experiences ought to be in optimal balance.

As teachers, we can dismiss the specific science behind the theory while still appreciating that our students likely do have an ideal ratio between challenge and ease, achievement and disappointment. Again, there is no substitution for working dynamically with the unique student in front of you. It may be that the positive:negative ratio changes daily or depends on the subject at hand, but it's probably true that most of us work best when the positive outweighs the negative.

Understanding Feedback

Whenever we engage with the environment or some new piece of information, we get feedback. Feedback is simply cause and effect, and lets us know the outcome of our actions. As a teacher, however, you facilitate this process and give your student feedback that is deliberately intended to support, guide and encourage them. Feedback is information on how we are doing relative to our goal. It's like a conversation—it's in the back and forth that meaning emerges. It's simple: when a student knows what effect their actions are having overall, they can adjust themselves, ultimately improving their performance, self-evaluation and awareness.

Somewhere along the line, it became common to blandly throw a "great job!" at students, regardless of their performance. Empty or insincere praise is as useless, however, as handing out a grade with no elaboration on how it was determined. Giving good, actionable and meaningful feedback as a teacher is an art. It's all about *how* feedback is given, rather than the specific words or phrases. We've already seen that on balance feedback should probably be more in favor of the positive than the negative, but there are other characteristics of quality feedback.

- **Respect**. As a baseline, students should feel that they are treated with dignity and politeness, no matter who they are. This allows feedback to be received for what it is, rather than as an attack on the individual. For example, in a male-dominated workplace, feedback for a female employee will likely only be effective if she genuinely feels as though what she is told is really about her performance, and not the fact that she is female.

- **Timeliness**. Feedback should be given as close as possible to the event it relates to. For example, don't wait for two weeks to evaluate performance on a project; your feedback is unlikely to "stick." On that note, for feedback to be formative, it needs to be provided often and in small doses—a single big evaluation can leave students feeling in the dark in the meantime, and can give avoidable errors a chance to compound.

- **Be specific.** You want your student to know exactly where they stand, and why. Vague feedback can feel stressful and leave people feeling bad about themselves. Instead, be clear about exactly what the student is doing right, what needs improvement, how they're performing against others or a fixed standard and, most importantly, the concrete steps they can take to remedy the situation. If a student simply feels they've been insulted or put down, they won't have any idea on what to do next, or how to improve.

- **Use the "sandwich" method.** A useful structure to follow is to begin with a compliment, move onto the correction, then end with a compliment. This way the feedback is cushioned in a context of positivity more likely to inspire and encourage. For example, "Your opening was great, and you have excellent breath control. The high notes are still feeling a little unsteady, but you finished strong, particularly that last chorus." Naturally, the compliments have to be sincere!

- **Describe rather than evaluate.** "Showing your work here has made it so much easier to follow your process" is more effective feedback than, "Hey, nice job showing your work." The difference is subtle, but the first encourages internal motivation and explains *why* something is being perceived favorably. The student can come to their own conclusions, and feel a more genuine pride than if they had merely been told "you're great!" Similarly, focus feedback on actions, skills or abilities, rather than personal attributes. This encourages a growth mindset that increases tolerance for failure and mistakes. So, saying "the follow-through on your backstroke is really getting stronger" is actually more likely to instill confidence than "you're a naturally gifted swimmer," which doesn't give the student much to work with. Avoid advice ("you should do XYZ") for the same reason.

- **Don't make it personal**. If a student is particularly sensitive, you can find ways to offer feedback without even referring to them directly. Model incorrect performance and then critique yourself, or talk about a hypothetical example.

Depending on your students' personalities, it may also work to ask them to evaluate themselves, or even give you feedback on your teaching—this makes the learning process feel like a mutual collaboration rather than a power dynamic with the teacher evaluating the student. For the same reason, avoid feedback explaining how pleased or upset you personally are by your student's performance—it's not about you!

- **Mix it up**. You can give feedback in a variety of ways. Pay attention to what works for your student and tailor your communication so it has the best chance of being heard. Consider again your student's innate motivators and appeal to those when giving feedback; for example, you may emphasize the relative ranking of a performance if you know your student is motivated by mastery and winning. Try giving feedback verbally, but also leave notes, or small, unobtrusive written corrections. Sometimes, a simple smile or thumbs up does the job. You could even get feedback from a third party that you look at together with your student.

Even if you're friendly, reasonable and transparent in your feedback, try to remember that criticism can *still* be difficult to stomach, so be kind. Try to strike a balance between sincerity and compassion, and avoid overwhelming your student by dumping lots of information on them all at once.

Giving feedback is about making realistic adjustments to learning, but it's also an emotional experience, so be mindful of this and give your student space to process what you've told them in their own way. If you never deliver feedback with an air of judgment, your student will quickly learn not to take it that way. One method for encouraging this neutral mindset is to put the feedback to use. Good feedback should be **actionable**. Ask your student to tell you how they plan to or have already incorporated your suggestions. This is empowering and can focus the mind, allowing the student to quickly move on from any potential feelings of embarrassment or disappointment.

Even better, when you link feedback to meaningful action, you get to see trends unfolding—the next time you evaluate your student, you could give them what might be the most satisfying piece of feedback of all: "I can see that you took that feedback from before and really ran with it, and because of your hard work you've definitely improved. Well done." For every piece of feedback you give, try to build in an opportunity to respond to that feedback and actually make meaningful changes.

Good feedback has a way of helping the student internalize their own ability to self-evaluate and adjust after observation. It teaches them how to think of their own progress. No matter what feedback you give or when, positive language can be extremely powerful. Again, it's not exactly *what* you say, but *how* you say it. Good feedback contains concrete and specific details to anchor the student in action, but it also contains an emotional component. Your choice of words communicates your respect, support and positive regard for the student.

Instead of saying, "I can't hear a word you're saying," go with "I can hear your voice so much better when you lift your chin and speak up like that. Then your passion in the speech really comes through."

Instead of saying, "This painting is just a mess," you could say, "I don't think your attempt to bring these elements together has really worked this time, and I have a feeling you didn't fully convey your meaning with your use of color here."

Rather than saying, "The reason you keep injuring yourself is because of your grip on the bat," you could say something like, "What do you think is the effect of holding your bat like that? What do you think would happen if you tried holding it a little higher up?"

Feedback is not the same as **advice**, and it's not the same as **evaluation**. To simply pronounce something good or bad doesn't actually help your student learn or improve. Think about your role in giving feedback as a facilitator of a natural process in life—i.e. we act, our actions have results, and if we want to learn we'd better notice these results and adjust accordingly. Draw attention to the effect of your student's actions, and relate it to the goal. Done *continuously and consistently*, your student is given ample opportunity to actually dig into the material and refine their understanding and their skill. When in doubt, favor feedback over teaching (i.e., the integrative approach to pedagogy).

To check your own skill at providing feedback, regularly ask yourself the following questions:

    a. Does my feedback refer to the goal? Feedback is more focused when it can basically answer the question, does the action I'm evaluating bring the student closer to or further from their stated goal? (Again we see why it's so important to have clearly stated goals in learning. Sometimes, simply reminding your student of the bigger aim is enough of a course correction.)

b. Is your feedback specific, concrete and actionable? Have you given guidance or observations that the student can genuinely do something with? For example, it's no use criticizing your student for not performing beyond what they are genuinely capable of. Keep judgments, assumptions and expectations out of feedback and look at plain, neutral facts, and precisely what to *do* given the feedback.

c. Is your feedback appropriate for your unique student? Feedback is communication, and communication fails if it's not received properly. Are you speaking in a way that is understandable for your student?

d. Does your feedback contain meaningful information on the task, the process, or the performance? In other words, are you offering information which genuinely provides insight and a learning opportunity?

Good feedback:

- is clear, purposeful, meaningful and compatible with prior knowledge
- is focused on the learning intention and success criteria
- occurs *as* students are doing the learning; therefore, verbal feedback is much more effective than written
- provides information on how and why the student has or has not met the criteria
- provides strategies for improvement

According to John Hattie, a prominent education researcher, feedback is useful when it addresses the fundamental questions of "where am I going?", "how am I going?" and "where to next?" These questions are powerful as they reduce the gap between where the student is, and where they are meant to be, in reference to their learning goals. Another form of powerful feedback is that sought by the teacher—where students show the teacher what they have learned (formative assessment).

As part of our explicit teaching culture, teachers regularly provide instructive feedback during the "we do" and "you do" phases. Importantly, explicit instruction often emphasizes the positive function of errors—when teachers make immediate corrections to ensure achievement of learning goals. This type of "error training" can lead to higher performance in classrooms if the teacher has created a safe environment in which students are comfortable in taking risks.

Teachers also use student assessment data, and seek feedback from students in lesson plenaries, as a source of feedback on the effectiveness of their teaching practice. Feedback is also sought from students in our 360-degree performance improvement process.

In the 2017 IPS Review Findings, the reviewers stated: "Discussions with student leaders showed that the setting of achievement goals and the ongoing provision of feedback from teachers about their performance was having a powerful and positive impact on their learning."

Takeaways

- Students will only learn when they are motivated, so it's a teacher's duty to establish a learning environment that supports this motivation.
- Humans take action according to their appraisal of the level of effort required, its likely outcome, and the perceived desirability of that outcome. Teachers can motivate students by increasing the perceived value of the learning goal and its process, as well as boosting expectation of a positive outcome without undermining intrinsic motivation.
- Gamification is an approach where gaming elements are brought into non-gaming contexts, like learning. Teachers can use "level-up" scaffolding, put the "player" in control of play, encourage strategic collaboration, and make sure that the student not only receives immediate feedback for every action, but that their play is always guided by a well-understood purpose and expectation of the "rules."

- Academic buoyancy is something that teachers should always encourage in students, and this consists of composure, confidence, coordination, commitment, and control. With a mindset that fosters the development of these traits, the difficult aspects of learning are overcome and mastered as surely as the material itself.
- Productive failure is the perspective that failure itself is a valuable teacher, and can enhance understanding and mastery more than success can. Teachers can model an optimal attitude to failure—i.e. that it is normal, manageable and indeed useful.
- Good teachers should create a learning atmosphere free from judgment. This means disconnecting performance from the student's self-worth or identity, so that failure and mistakes are not perceived as threatening or humiliating. When a teacher models nonjudgment, a student feels safe to explore, experiment and make purposeful mistakes on their learning journey.
- Feedback is a vital part of the student environment. Good feedback is concrete,

specific to the goal in question, timely, meaningful, relevant and understandable to the student, and comes with clear and realistic steps for next actions. It is not judgment, advice, praise or criticism without meaningful elaboration on the learning process itself.

Summary Guide

INTRODUCTION

- The effectiveness of teaching depends on the characteristics of the teacher, of the student, of the material being taught, and most importantly, on the way it is taught.
- There are five main theoretical approaches to teaching called pedagogical approaches. Pedagogy is the theory and practice of teaching. No single approach is the right one—rather, it's a question of fit between the teaching style and the student, material, teacher, learning goals, context, and level of understanding.
- The constructivist approach attempts to support learning as they construct knowledge piece by piece, building on what they already know in a sequential,

logical, and ordered fashion. The teacher's job is to chart an incremental course through a curriculum, promoting students to advance gradually.

- The collaborative approach takes advantage of the power of interpersonal relations to drive learning and understanding. The teacher can use collaboration, group activities, teamwork, dialogue, or student teaching to help students grasp new concepts.

- The inquiry-based approach has the teacher set up an environment that supports and encourages the student's curiosity, using questions to spur understanding. The student is given case studies, scenarios, and problems, or simply prompted to ask or answer questions, to shape their learning process.

- The integrative approach draws connections across disciplines and subjects to deepen understanding. By cross-pollinating experience and knowledge, students develop better understanding and recall, and enjoy a more applied approach to the concepts they learn.

- Finally, the reflective approach is about encouraging the student's innate self-assessment and metacognition, i.e. thinking about their own learning so that they can self-regulate and adjust, gaining insight. Teachers can encourage this by asking students to observe their position, analyze it, and then generate their own assessments to drive follow-up actions.
- The five approaches can be blended and modified as necessary.
- The approaches all share some fundamental assumptions, namely that good teaching is inevitably collaborative, facilitative, applied, student-centered, and flexible.

CHAPTER 1. TEACHER MINDSET

- John Hattie is an educational researcher whose meta-study aims to find the most effective teaching approaches and methods. This focus on evidence-based teaching is grounded in what has greatest benefits for student learning.

- Hattie found that there were six main characteristics associated with good teachers and good student outcomes.
- Passion for students' learning was by far the most important, and entailed a teacher being genuinely enthusiastic in the process of learning and their subject, which rubs off on students and inspires them to learn.
- Flexibility is also important, since it allows teachers to adapt and adjust to their unique students and their changing needs. A good teacher can observe the results of the lesson and change the pace, pedagogical approach, activities, tone, or feedback style accordingly, for their students' benefit.
- Clarity is what allows teachers to outline and communicate a clear, logical learning path for the student, and communicate this so that the student always knows what, why, and how they are learning. Clarity in feedback and expectations can make students feel secure and confident in their path.
- Good teacher-student relationships are also essential. A teacher needs to have a

genuine human connection with the student, and convey empathy and understanding. Like any relationship, it needs to be built on mutual respect, trust, and good communication.

- Good teachers are pragmatic and use only evidence-based teaching strategies. They are willing to learn, adjust, or try new things when old techniques aren't working. They hold themselves to high standards.

- The final characteristic is the desire and willingness to improve our teaching skills. A good teacher knows never to rest on their laurels, but to keep learning, keep refining their approach, and to work with other teachers to improve themselves continually.

CHAPTER 2. GENERAL PRINCIPLES FOR TEACHING AND EDUCATING

- No matter your subject, your lesson plan, or the age and stage of your student, you can draw on several time-tested educational principles.

- The Goldilocks principle is very intuitive: we should pitch the difficulty of our lessons "just right"—where they won't be too difficult nor too easy; some researchers have found this golden middle zone at the place the student has eighty-five percent success with the task. This theory is related to the Yerkes-Dodson law, which describes a non-linear relationship between arousal and performance. Our job as teachers is to know our students and adjust difficulty so they are always optimally challenged but not overwhelmed.

- It can be difficult to truly know when a student understands something, so we have to use questions and infer from their answers their level of understanding. Heick's taxonomy is a list of isolated tasks that increase in complexity. If your student can complete these tasks, you can assume they possess understanding at that level.

- There are six domains to tests understanding: the parts, the whole, interconnectedness, the function, the abstraction, and the self. You can test understanding using activities or direct questions, although not all tasks require understanding at all six levels.

- Clear communication is obviously essential. A lot depends on your ability to explain concepts to your students. The first step is to give a clear and delineated definition of the concept, and then to carefully use analogies, examples, elaborations, and metaphors to guide your student towards understanding.
- A teacher needs to be on guard for logical fallacies in their students in their quest to help them cultivate better critical thinking skills. By using pointed questions (i.e. the Socratic method) teachers can draw attention to fallacies such as ad hominem, straw man, false dilemma, and causal errors. Questions can be of many different kinds and can encourage students' self-awareness, reflection, and metacognition.

CHAPTER 3. VISIBLE LEARNING

- Educational researcher John Hattie synthesized 1200 teaching studies to form a meta-study examining the influence of different aspects on student learning outcomes. He ranked around 138 according to their effect, and believed that good teachers should commit to evidence-based approaches.

- Surprisingly, the biggest influence on student learning has to do with teacher attitudes: when teachers collectively believe in their efficacy as teachers, students benefit.
- Students benefit when they can self-grade, rather than being graded externally by a teacher. This allows students to take responsibility and ownership over their learning and develop self-awareness and insight. They're also usually quite accurate!
- Metacognition has great effects on student outcomes. Teachers can encourage students to think about their thinking and self-reflect on the cognitive tasks they are performing, over and above the content of the task.
- Tackling student difficulties directly can have the biggest effect on outcomes, i.e. teachers should work closely with

struggling students or those with learning disabilities. They can do this by intervening as soon as possible and assessing the effect of that intervention regularly.

- Teachers are likely to have more success if they pitch their lessons at the right developmental level. Students differ in their formal operational cognitive ability, i.e. the capacity for abstract thought. Teachers can adjust levels of abstraction and observe their students, so their lessons respect their developmental stage.

- Finally, students seem to learn best with jigsaw-style exercises that encourage group cooperation, interaction and communication. The teacher can combine this with self-reflection and metacognition to anchor and summarize the lesson at the end.

CHAPTER 4. STUDENT MINDSET

- Students will only learn when they are motivated, so it's a teacher's duty to establish a learning environment that supports this motivation.

- Humans take action according to their appraisal of the level of effort required, its likely outcome, and the perceived desirability of that outcome. Teachers can motivate students by increasing the perceived value of the learning goal and its process, as well as boosting expectation of a positive outcome without undermining intrinsic motivation.

- Gamification is an approach where gaming elements are brought into non-gaming contexts, like learning. Teachers can use "level-up" scaffolding, put the "player" in control of play, encourage strategic collaboration, and make sure that the student not only receives immediate feedback for every action, but that their play is always guided by a well-understood purpose and expectation of the "rules."

- Academic buoyancy is something that teachers should always encourage in students, and this consists of composure, confidence, coordination, commitment, and control. With a mindset that fosters the development of these traits, the difficult aspects of learning are overcome and mastered as surely as the material itself.

- Productive failure is the perspective that failure itself is a valuable teacher, and can enhance understanding and mastery more than success can. Teachers can model an optimal attitude to failure—i.e. that it is normal, manageable and indeed useful.

- Good teachers should create a learning atmosphere free from judgment. This means disconnecting performance from the student's self-worth or identity, so that failure and mistakes are not perceived as threatening or humiliating. When a teacher models nonjudgment, a student feels safe to explore, experiment and make purposeful mistakes on their learning journey.

- Feedback is a vital part of the student environment. Good feedback is concrete, specific to the goal in question, timely, meaningful, relevant and understandable to the student, and comes with clear and realistic steps for next actions. It is not judgment, advice, praise or criticism without meaningful elaboration on the learning process itself.

22818616R00116